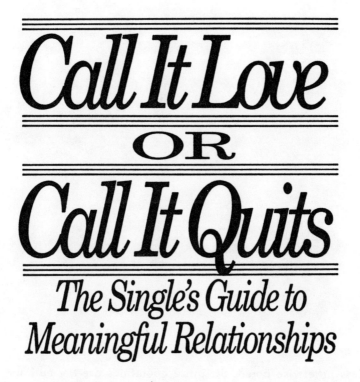

Call It Love
OR
Call It Quits

The Single's Guide to Meaningful Relationships

Tim Timmons
Charlie Hedges

WORTHY
PUBLISHING
FORT WORTH, TEXAS 76137

Copyright © 1988 by Worthy Publishing, Fort Worth, Texas 76137.

Library of Congress Catalog Card Number 88-50489

ISBN 0-8344-0175-4

10 9 8 7 6 5 4 3 2 1

To Janet and Milton Bennett, whose commitment to loving relationships provided the inspiration for this work.

To Carol Timmons, the better half of our oneness.

To Pam Hedges, who is for me the grace and love of God.

Contents

1

Be the One

Over 40 percent of the adult population in America is single. In Orange County, California, 43 percent of the people are single and over the age of twenty-two! This uncommonly high percentage of single people is reasonably easy to explain. People are simply waiting longer to get married. They are waiting for a number of different reasons: to finish their education, to become established in their careers, to attain a certain economic base. People are also waiting because they want to be wise: they don't want to make the same mistakes that others have made, they don't want to become a divorce statistic. (Divorce, itself, has significantly added to the singles' ranks.)

With so many single people running around, you would think that America could be just one great party. Right? Hardly. With so many single people running around we have the spread of America's biggest religion, "Confusionism." One of the key doctrines of confusionism is dating. Hardly anything is more wonderful and more weird than dating. I know. I spent fifteen years dating, and not dating—wishing I was when I wasn't, and wishing I wasn't when I was.

Why does dating have to be so weird? Why date anyway? Why not just forget the whole thing and stay single? Why not? Because we are created to be relational beings, because *life is relationship*. Without meaningful relationships our lives are incomplete. In one of his great essays, C.S. Lewis said, "Man alone is only possibility." We need people. We need relationships. And we greatly desire a meaningful relationship that might lead to marriage. But in the age of confusionism, how do we find the right person? Is there a secret or ten proven steps or a magical formula? No, but there is wisdom, and that's what this book is all about.

Meaningful relationships don't just magically happen. In spite of what we are often led to believe, meaningful relationships are not made up merely of mystery, magic, chemistry and fireworks.

We would like to think that somewhere "out there" is the perfect person who is just waiting for us, dying to meet us so that our lives could finally have meaning—kind of a "match made in heaven." But the truth of the matter is there simply are no matches made in heaven—at least not in the way that some think. Some of us have been told that when God made us he also made another person just for us, but, in an effort to make life more challenging, he hid them. Our task in life then is to find that other person. Some folks get lucky and find their partners by age twenty. Others are a little slower and don't find their mystical mates until age thirty. The real slow ones manage it by age forty, and then there are those who just can't seem to get the cosmic scheme together and so are doomed to loneliness.

This line of reasoning is totally erroneous. It ignores the fact that we are each responsible agents. And it undermines the very process by which we can discover and develop meaningful relationships. There are no perfect matches that have been cosmically preplanned to relieve us of the hard work it takes to develop a relationship. There are only matches that have developed through a process—a process of nurtured care, commitment and trust.

Successful relationships are the result of hard work, patience and process—three elements in which we have some choice and some control. That's good news because it means that we have some control in the result of this crazy thing we call intimacy, love, friendship . . . life. It is comforting to know that we have some say in the outcome of our relationships. We don't have to depend solely on the arrival of Mr. or Ms. Right.

Personness, Process and Permanence

After thousands of combined hours of marital and premarital counseling, and after a lot of personal experience, Tim Timmons and I have concluded that there are three major concerns for the development of a healthy relationship that might lead to marriage. These three concerns are personness, process and permanence. Around these three concerns we have structured this book.

Before you find the one, you must first *be the one*. That is the idea of personness. Many of our relationships fail, not because the other person didn't work out, but because we didn't work out. Life really is a journey in which we are constantly growing, learning, transforming. If our growth is stunted for some reason, it will affect our relationships with other people. It will affect our dating relationships. I once counseled the most eligible bachelor imaginable. He was in his early thirties, never married, wealthy, ridiculously good-looking, very bright, and lonely. At first glance, it would appear that he could be married anytime he wanted to. But that was not the case. There were some areas of personal growth he had yet to develop. He had to work on personness. The first section of the book will help you to identify some important issues of personal growth.

The second section is about the process. If relationships don't just magically happen, then how do they happen? Why do some relationships lead to marriage and others die before they even get going? Every healthy relationship will go through certain predictable stages of development. Our study of this process will outline and define what those stages are all about. In this section you may find the most helpful information that is available about dating. It is not a simplistic "how to" approach; it is a wisdom approach, composed of reason, not rules. How can you know if you should, or should not, marry someone? We will look at a way to answer that question.

In the section on personness, we talk about the individual before he or she becomes part of a couple; in the section on process, we discuss how a couple gets together; in the section on permanence, we describe how a couple stays together. Before you "call it quits," you need to evaluate what some experts call "the glue" of a relationship. Permanence is about commitment and conflict. They interplay off of each other. Every relationship has serious conflicts. The question is, what do we do with them? Is the commitment strong enough to keep us working through the conflict? There are few words in the English language that cause more craziness than the word commitment. What is commitment all about? How can we fight commitment phobia? How can we get to the point where we can make a lasting commitment?

Throughout the entire book we will deal with communication—how we reveal ourselves to others and how we receive others' revelations about themselves. How important is communication to a relationship? It is vital. Relationship is not built upon communication, nor is communication merely an integral part of relationship. But relationship *is* communication—open, honest and intimate.

We all are in need of meaningful relationships. They do not necessarily have to come in the form of a dating relationship, or even marriage. We find them in several different types of friendships, and much of the information in this book is acutely relevant to friendships. But the purpose of this book is to talk about dating—not just dating in general, but dating with a view toward the lifelong commitment of marriage.

Many of us are tired of playing at relationship. We're tired of the dating scene. We're tired of the guessing game that is involved in dating. This book will help to minimize the guessing and maximize the process of finding the one for you. You will have a better idea of when a relationship is right, and when it is not. You will know when to call it love or call it quits.

2

The Male-Female Quest

Ever since woman was split out of man, the male-female quest for a mate has been a powerful reality. The attraction for male-female action is probably the strongest of human desires. In fact, it's an irreversible attraction that breaks down all natural barriers including financial, cultural, racial and geographical barriers. It breaks down differences in personalities, age and physical appearance.

This incredible urge to merge back together is first detected at an early age. It starts out something like "Do you like Jimmy? Jimmy says he likes you." Then, "Are you going with Jimmy?" (although no one actually goes anywhere with anyone yet). Next, it's group dating and then dating. At this point, "going with" moves to "going out with" because now we really are going somewhere. Then dating becomes "getting serious," or "getting involved," then engagement and maybe even marriage. All of this for that insatiable quest for a significant relationship with a person of the opposite sex.

But the discovery of a significant relationship doesn't stop the quest as one might think. The male-female quest continues, even in the midst of a meaningful relationship. Within a relationship, the quest can be a fulfilling adventure of living and experiencing life's trials and joys together. Unfortunately, for too many relationships the male-female quest becomes instead a male-female quirk. One partner or the other (or both) become frustrated, discouraged and dissatisfied. Consequently, the relationship either dissolves or becomes a living stagnation.

How can we prevent such tragedy from occurring in our lives? I am convinced that one of the best ways to have a meaningful relationship with someone else is to begin by working on yourself. Before you find the one, you must first be the one!

Personal Hurdles to Happiness

In over fifteen years of counseling, I have never seen a male-female relationship work satisfactorily unless there were two individually happy people in the first place. Each person must be functioning properly (not perfectly) as a unique human being and contributing his or her uniqueness to the other person. Then a unique and healthy relationship is created naturally.

Although the plan for unique and healthy relationships is quite sensible, it is not so simple. There are three giant hurdles in everyone's way: the hurdle of maturity, the hurdle of communication and the hurdle of purpose.

The Hurdle of Maturity

Everyone who wants to relate well with the opposite sex must first grow up. Probably the most important aspect of growing up is realizing that *life doesn't revolve around us*. This is difficult to do because our lives do revolve around us. Think about it. Everywhere we go, we are there. Everything we do, we are there. Everyone we talk to, you guessed it, we're there, too. But in spite of what our individual experience may tell us, *life* does not revolve around us. There are others in the world who are just as important as we are.

Immaturity in one partner can stunt the growth of the relationship. It threatens the process of growing up together. When one outgrows the other in a relationship, "good reasons" for criticizing, resenting and pulling away from the other inevitably arise.

Years ago I met Jerry and Sarah at a Christmas party. Jerry was the life of the party. I really enjoyed his antics. Sarah seemed to enjoy Jerry's party antics as well, until dinner began. And then Sarah threw several sharp verbal darts his way that embarrassed us all. Jerry, in his quick, perceptive way, always seemed to recover, but I went away feeling bad toward Sarah and sympathetic toward Jerry. In only a few months, Jerry and Sarah were in the counseling room seeking my help.

As it turned out, immaturity was the problem, and Sarah was the burned out audience of one who just couldn't handle it any longer. Jerry was always the life of the party. Everyone liked Jerry. Sarah, too, had been drawn to him at a fraternity party in college. But as their relationship grew, Sarah discovered that she wanted a loving partner—a real grown-up man in her life. Jerry's M.O. was to be the life of the party, and since life isn't always a party, Jerry's "life" had been slowly dying out. Jerry still wanted to play the role of Peter Pan, and he wanted Sarah to play the part of Wendy. Without new insight there is very little chance Jerry will ever grow up!

For some, the hurdles of maturity are just too difficult to overcome. Either they're too painful or too confining. But without maturity, relationships go nowhere. Life goes nowhere!

The Hurdle of Communication

The second giant hurdle is communication. Maturity is the raw material you bring into a relationship. It's the "you"—the substance of who you are. Communication is the *skill* you bring into a relationship. It's "the expression of you"—the authentic presentation of who you are.

All relational problems come down to communication problems. There are no exceptions. Communication problems come in three flavors—none (or too little), improper (negative or abusive) and out of sync (poor listening). But no matter the flavor of the problem, the ultimate responsibility for poor communication falls on each person individually. Everyone must learn and work at it personally.

When there is little or no communication, many problems are set up in the relationship. The most obvious problem is that the relationship has little chance of making it in the first place. A relationship with little communication is unlikely to survive, and it is actually better that it doesn't. If a relationship with little communication does happen to proceed into marriage, disaster is inevitable.

When there is little or no communication in a marriage the so-called "mid-life crisis" is set up perfectly. The "mid-life crisis" occurs after a prolonged period of noncommunication. One person hasn't fully expressed what he or she feels (his or her wants, opinions, needs, etc.) and has slipped into an inauthentic role. This person will not stay in this role forever but will eventually wake up and explode. "I'm tired of being the glorified taxicab driver, PTA leader, women's club volunteer, part-time maid and chef, and full-time coordinator of the entire family. It's about time I do something for me!" Or "I'm sick of being the corporate climber, the community coach, the family paycheck and the one responsible for everything and everybody. It's about time I do something for me!"

This entire crisis could have been avoided through communication. Whose fault was it? Primarily the person now in crisis who rarely, if ever, communicated what he or she really felt.

The problem of improper communication is exposed when conflict is present. Improper communication seldom allows for resolution. In premarital counseling I always look for conflict and how it is resolved. There are two obvious roadblocks. Either there is no conflict, or the conflict that is there is unresolved. If there is none, that tells me either one or the other is already dead or that the conflict has been suppressed. Instead of exploding outwardly, one explodes inwardly. This unexpressed internal explosion is called imploding. Imploding builds up pressure for later volcanic activity which could blow everyone's head off.

The second roadblock is unresolved conflict. In this case, the explosions are quite visible, but resolution of the conflict that caused the explosion rarely happens. In this relationship everyone must walk through mine fields, carefully watching every step. Conflict is not a problem, but unresolved conflict will destroy relationships. Only healthy communication will solve this problem.

Out-of-sync communication will continually distance two people in a relationship. Each time you do not listen carefully to the other person your communication is out of sync. When someone talks to you, you must listen and talk back on the same wavelength. However, each time you do not clearly communicate back on the same wavelength, you place a brick between you and the other person. Your relationship can handle only so many bricks before a wall is built up between you. Then you have to resort to yelling over the wall, bursting through it or just walking away from it.

Communication done properly and in sync with another person is not reserved only for the specifically gifted. It's a hurdle anyone can learn to get over.

The Hurdle of Purpose

The third giant hurdle is purpose. Maturity is the substance of who you are. Communication is the expression of who you are. Purpose gives direction to who you are. Where are you going with your life? This personal dimension is part of every relationship, too.

A few years ago, I counseled one of those "perfect" couples. They had been dating for about a year and looked terrific together. They enjoyed the same activities. Their communication was exceptional. But Jim and Erica were splitting up. Erica called to talk with me alone. She had discovered why she was so resistant to Jim, and she wanted to verify her discovery with me. "Jim isn't going anywhere. He's in a great position in his company but is unhappy with his job. He seems lost as to what he wants to do with his life." Jim had never made it over the hurdle of purpose. He was lost and she sensed it.

The hurdle of purpose doesn't require great detail, but it does require direction. It's so difficult to make a permanent commitment to someone who is unsure of his or her direction.

Now there is one other danger with the hurdle of purpose. A person may have discovered and defined well his or her direction, but there is a large gap between the "talk" and the "do." You see, even if you're on the right track, you may still be run over if you just sit there.

Jumping the Hurdles

We seem to feel that each of these hurdles can be easily overcome—that maturity, communication and purpose eventually will just happen. However, in order to win the prize, something must be spent. In this case, the prize is a long-term relationship, and the basic cost is jumping these personal hurdles.

Just as there are many who have become expert fumblers when it's time to pay the check at dinner, too many people fumble away at picking up the check on maturity, communication and purpose. Most people will do anything to avoid the painful price tag attached to these hurdles. So what makes people pick up the check? What makes people jump?

It's been my experience that most people jump over these personal hurdles only when forced to do so. It can occur with the utter realization that "I am going to lose the person I love if I don't get my act together." Some people have to come to the end of themselves, to hit bottom. For others, it takes a tragedy to motivate them: personal injury, financial crisis, a relational rejection or breakup, an accident, a hospital experience, a life-threatening disease, the loss of a loved one. *Tragedy will often serve as a wake up call.*

A wake up call can also come from the confrontation of family and friends. Some people need a little swift kick to the posterior region to motivate them to jump over these personal hurdles.

A few wake up on their own after gaining insight into themselves and personally decide to jump. Naturally, this is the most desirable of all.

Each of the personal hurdles—maturity, communication and purpose—requires significant energy and effort from us. There is no arrival point, but in each hurdle an on-going process is necessary.

The Hurdle of Maturity—Grow Up

Maturity is working through frustrations. It's breaking through the impasses in our way. It's moving from dependence into independence. Your first gasp for air at birth was an impasse—to breathe or not to breathe. Break through that impasse by breathing and you will grow. Choose to remain totally dependent upon mom and you will die.

Each of the frustrations of life must be handled in order for us to mature: walking, talking, playing with friends, staying with babysitters, going to preschool and school, etc. Immaturity results when a person is protected or shielded from having to work through these frustrations of life. We spoil kids and adults when we bail them out or handle difficulties for them. Our society is filled with this kind of immaturity that makes for great difficulty in relationships.

Maturity is a lifelong process. We are continually in the process of arriving. As I have observed, there are at least four learning processes which must be operating for a person to blossom into maturity.

First, *learn to be agreeable without making false agreements.* Most relational problems are not caused by our conflicts, but by agreements we really didn't mean to make. As we enter into these false agreements, our true feelings are suppressed in order to go along with the flow. It's easier to go along and make everyone happy than to blow the whistle and stand alone. Each false agreement is made for fear of the horrible consequences that might come from being authentic and truthful. "If I were to call off the wedding, my mother would suffer cardiac arrest!" "There's no way I could even express how I really feel about that now. It's too late and it would destroy everything!" False agreements underlie dating relationships, engagements, marriages, business arrangements, etc. Every false agreement sets up either long-term disappointment or a sudden shock or snapping when the one who has made the false agreement wakes up enough to tell the truth.

False agreements are the product of immaturity. If you are going to grow and jump over the hurdle of maturity, you must learn to be agreeable without making false agreements. Learn to stand alone on the merit of your own feelings and opinions!

Second, *learn to take personal responsibility for your life.* Possibly our society's most-loved pastime is to blame someone or something for whatever is going wrong. We have become expert "blame throwers." We blame the past, parents, mates, drugs, secretaries, lack of money, machinery breakdown, the "other" woman, alcohol, God, traffic and any other convenient target. It's as natural as breathing!

Although your misfortune may be the fault of something or someone else, what you do with the circumstances you have been dealt is up to you. Study after study confirms this. Two kids grow up in an alcoholic family. One lives a life of wreckage, and the other lives successfully. Two women go through a messy divorce. One lives her life weighted down with resentment and bitterness, and the other lives with joy, experiencing life as a new and fresh adventure. The difference is in the person, not the circumstances.

Third, *learn to face the pain now and avoid the disaster later.* The catastrophe that we believe will happen if we attempt to jump over the hurdle is stuffed with pain. And most of us avoid pain at all costs. But the avoidance of pain now will most definitely increase the pain we must face someday. It's like a balloon payment—always difficult, sometimes impossible!

Growing up is learning to do the painful, uncomfortable things of life when it's the responsible thing to do—the painful phone call or letter, the difficult confrontation or the uncomfortable confession. It's learning to hold ourselves accountable. If we are going to grow up and jump over the hurdle of maturity, we must learn to face the pain now and avoid the disaster later!

Fourth, *learn self-discipline rather than self-destruction.* The human species will do almost anything to avoid jumping over the hurdle of maturity, even self-destructive things. The pain of breaking through that wall of growing up just seems too much. So, many people "choose" to embrace an illness or attempt suicide rather than choose to jump the hurdles and grow up. Besides, when you are sick, hurt, unlucky or down and out, you can collect all kinds of loving strokes from the willing rescuers around you. Self-victimization will get you "everything" except maturity!

Self-destruction and maturity don't blend well at all. Instead of self-destruction try little doses of self-discipline. Scott Peck, in his book *The Road Less Traveled,* has defined discipline as "love translated into action." Self-discipline is love for ourselves translated into actions. Self-discipline is the exercise of self-control or self-strength. It's learning to do a few things (1) all by ourselves (2) depending on no one and (3) competing with no one. Some forms of exercise fit the self-discipline cri-

The Constitution of the United States guarantees free speech, but it does not guarantee an audience.

teria: walking, jogging, swimming, weight-lifting and aerobics. Self-discipline in eating can be a great experience as you learn what you can or cannot eat. Others exercise self-discipline in their personal study, note-writing, or quietly giving of their wealth to needy charitable organizations. If we are going to grow up and jump over the hurdle of maturity, we must learn self-discipline rather than self-destruction. We must experience self-strength and self-control!

The Hurdle of Communication—Speak Up

The Constitution of the United States guarantees free speech, but it does not guarantee an audience. Whether we have a listening audience or not depends upon the quality of our communication. Even though there are numerous courses on communicative skills and methods, quality will always be lacking unless we are able to communicate our authentic emotions—the true us.

Dr. Everett Shostrom, one of the "deans" of psychology, defines the emotions in quadraphonic: love, anger, weakness and strength. These primary feelings are at the core of our existence. As I have explored these for myself and others, I have discovered a new freedom in the communication of my true self.

Each of these emotions is connected to its opposite: love and anger, weakness and strength. They operate in polarity to each other. Polarities are like seasons. They follow a rhythm. In order to experience our weaknesses, we must feel our strengths. There is a time for feeling love and a time for feeling anger. It's difficult to love fully without a genuine expression of our anger. We feel anger primarily with those we love. Each of these emotions is neutral and privately owned. They are neither good nor bad, but they are genuinely ours.

There are three ways we can experiment with our communication so that it more adequately expresses our unique personness.

First, *experience your emotions.* I find that most people do not allow themselves to experience their own emotions authentically. We are admonished: "Stop being angry right now!" "Be careful of how you love!" "Don't act so weak!" "You're coming on too strong!" It's no wonder we suffer from emotional constipation!

Second, *express your emotions.* Fear holds us back from expressing our core feelings. Instead of communicating authentic feelings, we shift into a safer backup style. We manipulate with inauthentic feelings. Instead of expressing love we *please and placate.* Instead of showing anger we *blame and attack.* Instead of admitting weakness we *avoid and withdraw.* Instead of using strength we *dictate and control.* Avoid these manipulations like the plague. They will destroy genuine communication with another person.

Third, *encourage emotions in others.* Communication is two directional. The communication dynamic always involves at least one other. Once we begin to experience and express our authentic feelings, it is extremely difficult to step back and allow others the full expression of their authentic feelings.

The urge to fix people and their feelings is too great. When a person is weak, there is a temptation to fix him, to rescue him. When he is strong, there is a temptation to set him up for a fall. In order to get over this hurdle, we must possess our own feelings and allow everyone else to possess theirs. In other words, if a friend feels like having a royal hostilectomy with his anger, let him have it! Those are his feelings. He owns them. We choose to be or not to be affected by them. As we encourage others to speak up, we will find an increased strength to speak up for ourselves.

As in the hurdle of maturity, the hurdle of communication is a lifelong process. It involves listening, studying, attending seminars and workshops, and possibly personal counseling.

Call It Love or Call It Quits is another in a long list of contributions that will enhance your communication process. However you process it, if you are going to jump over the hurdle of communication, you must speak up!

The Hurdle of Purpose—Get Up

For too many people their get-up-and-go has gotten up and gone! For us to jump the hurdle of purpose, we must first get up and state a direction for our lives. This is a dynamic, rather then a static, direction. In it must be enough flexibility to take advantage of the unforeseen opportunities that come our way. Once we have experienced some growth and learned how to express our feelings more authentically, we will know much more about who we are. Then is the time to determine where we want to go.

Just be certain you are going somewhere. It's always easier to guide a moving object. Resurrection of the dead is nearly impossible at every level. Get up! Describe the general direction you want to go with your life. The more you talk about it the clearer it will become.

Second, if we want to jump over the hurdle of purpose, we must get up and do what we describe as our direction. There will always be direction corrections along the way, but we must follow through and do it. Plan your life and live your plan! Jumping over the hurdle of purpose will give us a sense of confidence that will show through in everything we do.

Grow up...and jump the maturity hurdle!

Speak up...and jump the communication hurdle!

Get Up...and jump the purpose hurdle!

Jumping all three hurdles is a personal matter. It's like taking a bath—no one can do it for us. We must jump each one all by ourselves. Years ago I learned that if you don't work on yourself all your life, everyone else will. And you will not like the finished product.

Jumping all three hurdles will create a greater authenticity to the expression of who we are as people. This, in turn, makes for a more authentic and workable male-female quest and consequently, a more authentic and workable, long-term relationship.

Before you find the one, you must first be the one. The most eligible daters are those people who are most comfortable with themselves. The most successful daters are those who have jumped the hurdles. Those are the ones who are prepared to work on a relationship because they know firsthand what it takes—a commitment to growth, personal and interpersonal.

3

The World According to You

On our way to meaningful relationships, our primary focus must not be on the other person until we have first prepared ourselves. Whether or not someone has that wonderful potential of being the "right" one for us is secondary to whether *we* have the wonderful potential of being the "right" one. In other words, we must be the right one before we find the right one.

Celebrate Your Uniqueness

Each person has a remarkable quality that differentiates him from all others. Similarity and equality are present, but sameness is not. A potter molds the clay to make 100 bowls. The similarities are there, and the differences are hardly distinguishable, but each one is different. God has created and molded people in the same way. There is no mass production upon an assembly line that cranks out the same old product day in and day out. No way! God, our Creator, has uniquely put his mark on each of us, and the uniqueness of each personality is like the fingerprint—one of a kind and never the same. And that unique personality is one of the special gifts from the God who created you.

Think of it! When your father deposited sperm into your mother to get your mother's egg, there were about two billion sperm. Two billion sperm after your mother's egg, and you

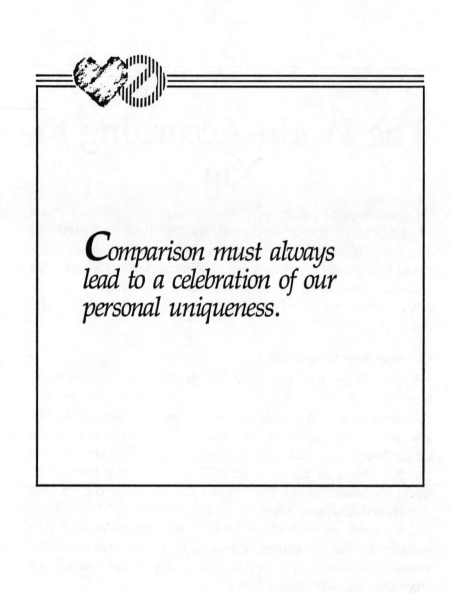

Comparison must always lead to a celebration of our personal uniqueness.

won! You beat out two billion "others" to become you! You are an unrepeatable miracle of God!

Celebrate the Differences

It's important that we understand and appreciate ourselves as unique individuals. We must be constantly discovering the world according to us. Each of us operates on the basis of different wants, beliefs, actions and emotions. We each operate on different channels. We express ourselves with differing themes, and we experience differing comfort levels.

And it's almost impossible to change our channels or themes. If you take the teeth out of a lion, he is still a lion—a toothless lion—and not a domesticated cat! Although we cannot change our channel or theme, we find it quite easy to attempt to change everyone around us. Why aren't people more like me? Why don't people do things the way they "should"? In other words, why don't they handle life the way I do? Our natural tendency is to make others over to live their lives the "right" way—our way! We have our personal projects— friends, dates, spouses, children, associates. But about all these projects produce is resistance in them and frustration in us!

Instead of trying to eliminate the differences, each of us must understand and appreciate the differences that make us who we are. Comparing ourselves is a necessary step, but we must be careful because comparisons can depress us. Don't get caught up in the comparison traps of "I'm better than she is!" or "I can't ever do it as well as he can!" Only compare in order to appreciate the differences, act on them in relationships and affirm your own uniqueness. Differences must never lock us up into life-competition with others, but they should help us define our uniqueness and how we can better relate to others. Comparison must always lead to a celebration of our personal uniqueness.

Personality Homes

One helpful way to understand better our similarities and differences is by looking at personality types. The two books that have been most helpful to me in understanding personality types and, therefore, have helped shape this chapter are *Please Understand Me; Character and Temperament Types* by David Keirsey and Marilyn Bates and *Gifts Differing* by Isabel Briggs Myers with Peter B. Myers.

Everybody has eight personality traits within them, and the combination of these traits creates a personality "home" within each person. The eight traits are divided into four pairs of traits: extroversion and introversion, sensing and intuition, thinking and feeling, judging and perceiving.

Sociability separates *extroversion* and *introversion*. Extroverts get their energy from people. They become more energized as the party goes on. They are more comfortable with people around them. Introverts need space. They get their energy from solitude. Parties may wear them out! They are more comfortable with time alone. This recharges their batteries. Extroverts feel lonely when all alone, but introverts experience loneliness in a crowd.

A misunderstanding here will be the seedbed for innumerable conflicts. The extrovert is concerned about the external and the extensive in his approach to life; the introvert is internal and intensive. Unfortunately, with most of our population posing as extroverts (approximately 75 percent), the introverts have taken the brunt of criticism. Neither one makes a better person in relationship with another. Each must be understood and appreciated in order to maximize our relationships.

Sensing and *Intuition* pertain to how people perceive life. Sensing people deal with actual facts. They tend to say exactly what they mean. They are capable of handling many details with instant awareness. Intuitive people deal with the possible facts—what might have, could have, would have been. They don't tell you what they really mean at first. Much of the time Intuitive people speak in code, not completing sentences and expecting people to understand what they mean. Sensing people take the facts at face value. Intuitive people analyze the facts behind the facts. When I say to my wife, who is intuitive, "I like that dress!", she will reply quizzically, "Why?"

Thinking and *Feeling* pertain to how people make decisions. Thinking people make decisions based upon logic and reasoning. Feeling people make decisions based upon a gut level feeling or value judgment. Thinkers can make a critical statement that makes sense but without great feeling behind it. Feelers easily become defensive and hurt. About 88 percent of men in the U.S. are Thinkers and 12 percent are Feelers. Conversely, 88 percent of women in the U.S. are Feelers and 12 percent are Thinkers. In other words, the Feeling man and the Thinking woman are rare and tend to shock us by their "rare" behavior as we try relating to them. It's no problem if you know. It may be devastating if you do not.

Judging and *Perceiving* pertain primarily to how you schedule your time. Judges like to be on time or even a little early. They live their lives on a schedule. They want decisions made and tasks completed. Perceivers are more flexible. Tomorrow is just as good as today for a task to be completed—maybe even preferable because of new information you might uncover tomorrow. With a deadline of 8:00 P.M., Judges will be there at 8:00 P.M. or before. For Perceivers, 8:00 is not a deadline, but a guideline.

Let's put these traits together. Check out especially your profile, but don't overlook each of the others. You will find many of your family and friends as you do. You may even be able to understand them and you better. Remember, the better you understand yourself, the better able you will be to find the right relationship for you.

Sensors/Perceivers

Sensors/Perceivers bring joy into our lives! They are action oriented. They live life as a gourmet feast. They spend life freely—always on the edge of adventure. There is always the sense that something exciting is about to happen! Work is essentially play for them. They make up approximately 38 percent of the population.

Sensors/Perceivers work best in a crisis and do not fill a maintenance role well. Defeat is only temporary to these people who are able to survive setbacks that would devastate others. They are spontaneous, living in the immediate. They are important and impulsive. For them to wait is psychological death.

Sensors/Perceivers are perfection in action. They don't like to practice but usually do their best in performance. They normally miss romantic nuances, neglecting a small word of affection. Yet they are masters of the grand gesture—the three-carat diamond, the two dozen roses or the mink coat!

In love relationships they tend to become involved quickly and then feel burdened by the relationship. They don't like courtships. They are basically uncritical with a happy disposition. They like surprises and love to give and receive gifts. They may seem like they don't need anyone at all, but they do. Although they are into whirlwind courtships, they tend to be loyal once the selection is made.

Sensors/Judges

Sensors/Judges bring order and a sense of duty to the world. They exist to be useful to the social units they belong to. To belong is imperative, but it must be earned. They are the caretakers of society, not the cared for. Whereas the Sensors/Perceivers are free and independent with a play ethic, the Sensors/Judges are bound and obligated with a work ethic. They have a keen sense for detecting ingratitude. They are parental. Their theme is the same as the Boy Scouts: be prepared. They have a pessimistic theme, expecting things to go wrong. Without a doubt, Murphy of Murphy's Law was a Sensor/Judge.

Sensors/Perceivers throw the party, and the Sensors/Judges do the work at the party. As the Sensor/Perceiver spends, the Sensor/Judge saves.

In love relationships Sensors/Judges are extremely loyal. Many are the Mother Theresas of our world. They express their affection in standard ways by verbalizing and bringing gifts. They are careful with their money and possessions, and their activities are orderly and preplanned. They make up approximately 38 percent of the population.

Intuitive Thinkers

Intuitive Thinkers bring us understanding and explanation. They have brought us science. They have a desire for powers—power over nature, power over numbers, power over ideas. They want to control, predict, understand and explain realities.

Intuitive Thinkers require competence from themselves and others. Capability, ability, capacity, skills and ingenuity are all Intuitive Thinker terms for doing things well under varying circumstances. They judge capabilities with ruthless self-criticism. They never believe that they know enough or do things well enough. They are perfectionists who become tense and compulsive in their behavior when under stress. You can always count on the end product (when it does arrive) to be excellent, well thought through and logical, with all possible options explored.

To the Intuitive Thinker, work is work and play is work. They know logically that recreation is necessary for health. Therefore, they will schedule their play and even demand that they have a good time.

Because of their passion for knowing and their search for

the whys of the universe, they are terrific listeners. On the other hand, they possess a reluctance to repeat things or to state the obvious. They are fascinated with words and their meanings.

In relationships they may seem aloof and uncaring. They don't ververbalize. They enjoy disputing intellectually but not quarreling emotionally. They need much time and energy invested in them. Social time is not of great importance to them. They are unaware of days and dates unless they are reminded.

On the whole they are rather serious. They take their family responsibility seriously. Promiscuity repels them, and they would never discuss their mates with others. They have a great capacity to enjoy without having to possess. They are satisfied with modest comfort, not possessions. They make up about 12 percent of the population.

Intuitive Feelers

Sensors/Perceivers, Sensors/Judges and Intuitive Thinkers all pursue ordinary goals, but Intuitive Feelers pursue the extraordinary. It's difficult for them to understand the "false" goals of everyone else. They are into becoming. Their purpose in life is to have a purpose in life. There is a hunger for self-actualization. They want to make unique contributions—to make a difference!

Intuitive Feelers are into meaningful pursuits! They are the ones who attend seminars, workshops and field trips. They are idealists and romanticists. They are always stretching into the future to define and design what might be. Whereas Intuitive Thinkers are principle oriented, Intuitive Feelers are people oriented.

In relationships Intuitive Feelers would rather die for love—the Romeos and Juliets of our world. They are motivated by the perfect love, by a spiritual relationship. They make charming, warm, supportive and understanding mates. They remember all important dates and tend to mark them with symbolic meanings. They give lavish gifts, but do so in private. They identify closely with their mates and want their mates to be in meaningful pursuits. They have great difficulty saying no. Intuitive Feelers, who make up about 12 percent of the population, add warmth, beauty and meaning to the world!

Compare Your Differences

At a Sunday morning church service the congregation's makeup is quite varied. Most likely, there will be more Intuitive Feelers than any other type. They want *inspiration*. They love the music or the minister to stimulate those goose bumps down the spine. Sensors/Judges want *ceremony*. They are more into tradition—normalcy. New or way-out things make them uncomfortable. Intuitive Thinkers show up for the *content*—theology. They want to be stimulated with ideas and words and logic! The Sensors/Perceivers want festivity—*celebration!* They want the experience to be enjoyable and fun, anything but boring.

You can also see the four types through each person's response to the policy manual at the office. Sensors/Judges will read it and believe it as the "business Bible." They want to do things properly and orderly. Intuitive Thinkers will read the manual and change it. And they make it better! Sensors/Perceivers may or may not read it, but if they do, they will only use what is practical. The Intuitive Feelers may or may not read it, but they love to get together and talk about it!

You and the other half of your potential relationship are remarkably unique. So what? One of the most vital ingredients of a meaningful relationship is the magic that results from the appreciation of differences. In order to accurately appreciate one another's differences, it is absolutely necessary to affirm one another's uniqueness. Take the time to understand yourself so that you can express your uniqueness most clearly. Help people understand the world according to YOU. Be the one before you find the one. Be the one and you *will* find the one!

4

Staging Your Relationship

I am convinced that nothing in the world is more confounding and confusing than relationships. And the confusion is heightened ten times when a relationship is a romantic one. Norm Wright, a famous marriage counselor, has said that it doesn't take long in a marriage to find out that you have married an alien. Well, many of us have discovered the same thing in our dating relationships. In fact, many readers of this book are probably convinced that there is life on other planets simply because they have dated Klingons, Venusians and Martians. I might have called this section of the book an "anti-cloaking device" or an alien detection section.

We all have great fears of getting into a bad relationship and ultimately of marrying into a bad relationship. We have all seen other people do it. In fact, most of us have been in one of those relationships. Don't you wish there was some guarantee in relationships? Don't you wish you could know for sure if you should marry someone? That is the purpose of this section of the book. I want to give you helpful information about "how to know for sure."

I believe this section could change your dating life. I won't offer any guarantees other than if you take the information seriously, your dating relationships will improve greatly. And, should a dating relationship lead to marriage, you will be able to enter marriage more confidently.

Communication experts agree that the development of

meaningful relationships is the result of a process, or stages. All relationships will travel along an intimacy continuum that moves from strangers to acquaintances to friends to lovers. This intimacy continuum is called the Stages of a Relationship. What we must learn is how to move wisely through those stages as a relationship grows. In this section you will discover how to stage your relationship wisely. You will recognize why some of your past relationships failed and why some went reasonably well.

There are four stages to relationships. Relationships begin with a "testing" period where the partners look for areas of similarity and mutual desirability. They then move to a period of "experimenting" and "negotiation" where the couple begins to intensify the degree of intimate communication. The third stage is one of "commitment," during which meaningful bonds are formed, and deeper trust is realized. The final stage is "institutionalizing" where a public declaration is made regarding the depth, breadth and longevity of the commitment.

Testing, negotiating, committing and institutionalizing are fine terms if you are a communications major. But I prefer to use English. I simply call them Hoping, Scoping, Coping and Roping: hoping this is the one, scoping out the one, coping with the one, and finally roping the one, or marriage. (In the middle of a seminar I was giving, one participant suggested that we call the final stage "moping." I think he understood the need well.)

As we discuss the stages of a relationship, keep in mind that the lines separating each stage are very soft. It is impossible to determine the exact moment when you leave one stage and enter another. There is a gray area of overlap between them. Also, keep in mind the purpose of this section is descriptive and not prescriptive. The purpose is not to prescribe or dictate how your relationship must grow. The idea is to describe the normal, healthy process of relational growth in order to help you make wise decisions as you go through the process yourself.

Successful relationships don't just magically happen. They are the result of work, patience and process—the process called the Stages of a Relationship.

5

Hoping

It was the summer before my final year in seminary. I had just driven up to a friend's house for a Saturday afternoon barbecue. As I got out of my car, I heard a woman's voice. "Hi. My name is Pam. You probably don't remember me, but we were briefly introduced about a year ago while I was visiting Portland." I looked up, and sure enough I didn't remember her. But we spent the rest of the afternoon (and evening) talking. I was enormously intrigued by her and made plans to see her again. Slightly more than a year later we were married.

As I look back on that night and the dates that were to follow, I wonder, "What was it about Pam that attracted me to her? Of all the people I had met, why was I so specially attracted to her?"

What about you? How many thousands of people have you met in your life? And isn't it curious that of all those people there were only a few that you had any desire to get to know better? Why is that so? The answer is found in the first stage of a relationship.

The first stage of a relationship is awkward, to say the least. The whole idea of dating is awkward. But, the most awkward part of dating is the first, second and third dates—what should we do, what should I wear, how should I act, will I enjoy myself, will my date enjoy himself or herself? When I was dating, my most common question was, "How did I get myself into this one?" Yet, there was something that did "get me into this one." What was it?

How do we begin to develop friendships? What makes us think that we might want to date someone? And what makes us want to date them a second, third or fourth time? These are some of the questions we deal with in the first stage of a relationship, the stage called Hoping.

Description of the Stage

In technical communication jargon the first stage of a relationship has been classified by several different names: testing, initiating, sampling. All of these terms point to the same idea—two people checking each other out, getting to know each other and deciding whether they might like to continue to grow as friends. In a dating relationship, it is two people hoping that this just might be a person they could get close to in a very special way.

The big idea in the Hoping Stage is discovery. Two people find out basic information about each other and discover areas of overlap. On the surface that basic information might look like a demographical survey: age, education, employment, hobbies, church. But the real nitty gritty of what the couple is trying to discover is "who is this person on the inside?" It is a search to discover the other person's values, interests, character and personality. The Hoping Stage is a process of intuitive discovery, which is complicated by a funny little animal called "our list."

Whether we admit it or not, all of us have hidden somewhere inside of us a list of what we want in a mate. This list is composed of traits that we desire (intelligence, humor, looks, integrity), as well as a collection of traits that we would absolutely reject (dominance, insensitivity, self-centeredness, untrustworthiness). Sometimes we are aware of our list, but most of the time we are not.

The list is a funny thing; it's there, but it's like a barely distinguishable vapor. We can sense it and feel it, but we can't touch it. And the moment we do try to touch it, it seems to float away. Yet, that doesn't make the list any less real or any less a major part of the Hoping Stage. The list is a key factor in this stage of a relationship because it represents a mirror image of ourselves—the qualities and traits that best complement us. The list is not unhealthy, in and of itself, but it can be destructive as will be discussed later in the chapter. Part of the discovery made in the Hoping Stage is to determine in a reasonably short period of time how this new person stacks up against our list.

In this Hoping Stage relationships can move from acquaintances to friends. What causes a relationship to deepen into a friendship? That's what we will look at in this chapter. Keep in mind that the idea here is more of a "how come" than a "how to."

Distinctives of the Stage

If the Hoping Stage is one of discovery, what is it we are trying to discover? It boils down to three items: commonality, rapport and potential complement. When we enter the Hoping Stage, we subconsciously ask three basic questions of the other person: 1. Do we have similar interests and values? (commonality) 2. How well do we get along? (rapport) 3. Do we have complementing strengths and weaknesses? (potential complement)

We are searching for areas of overlap. They are the areas of attraction, the things that draw us together in the first place. The greater the area of overlap the greater the possibility of growth in the relationship; on the other hand, if there is little overlap, the chances are slim for continued relationship. Let's look at the three critical areas for overlap: commonality, rapport and potential complement.

Commonality

It is vital to the success of a relationship that we have certain things in common. Surprisingly, items that we give much concern—demographics such as age, career, salary, dependents, education—often have less importance than we think. It's not that these items are unimportant, but they are only shadows of the real issues. The real issues consist of who people are down deep—their interests and values. Our individual demographics serve only as pointers to who we are inside. I may demographically hold a degree from a seminary, but that is far from who I am. I am a complex person with many attributes, only one of which is represented by a seminary education.

What should you be looking for in someone's demographics? The landmarks that point to a very important part of your new friend's personness: his or her guiding interests and governing values. A distinction needs to be made here between interests and values. Our interests guide us, but our values govern us. Our interests are things we like to do; our values are things we must do. You might be interested in becoming a public speaker, and your interest may move you to do so. But, your values will determine what you will speak about and the intensity with which you will speak. Your values will govern if you are to be a politician, an activist, a preacher or an entertainer. You may have an interest in becoming an attorney, and your interest may move you to do so. But your values—your values regarding money, justice, rights—will drive you to practice a certain brand of law.

The discovery of another person's interests and values is important because our interests and values describe much of who we are at our core. A question that frequently arises is, "Can I have a successful relationship with someone whose interests and values are different from mine?" My answer is found in another question, "How much different and in what way?" You will never find someone whose interests and values are identical with your own. It would be downright boring if you did. But, where is the line between attractively unique and incompatible? How different is too different? The answer to that lies within yourself, and you must evaluate personally the magnitude of the differences. Sometimes the differences are too great for the relationship to continue and other times the differences can even be healthy.

A couple of examples will help make the point. On our first date my future wife and I discovered that we were interested in some very different things. Our first date was composed of two parts, her part and my part. We began our date one mid-afternoon by going to an open-air arts and crafts festival. That was her idea. She loved it. We wove our way in and out of every little booth in the place. I practically slept through it. Who cares that some guy can make a ring out of a fork? or fifty of them! I thought it made for a pretty nondescript outing.

The next part of the date was the good part—my part. We went to a little avant-garde restaurant for dinner, followed by a foreign film (one with subtitles). I had a great time (the film is still one of my favorites). She, on the other hand, thought I was from Mars. She still laughs at the event by saying, "A foreign movie with subtitles? When I got home that night, I was convinced that he would never ask me out again and to tell the truth I didn't care." The point is my wife and I are different in some of our interests, but not irreconcilably so.

On the other hand, let's say that I had an avid interest in dirt-bike riding and camping, so avid that I had to be involved monthly or weekly. Now we would be approaching a possible problem area. My wife has less than no desire to ever become a camper, sleep outside, share a bathroom and leave her hair-drier at home. If this were the case, would it mean that we couldn't make it as a couple? Not necessarily. But we might have had a harder time getting together in the first place because our interests could have been perceived as being too different. Different interests are often reconcilable, but if they are radically different, it may be a warning sign for the couple.

However, when we talk about commonality in values, we enter a whole new arena. Remember, interests are things we like to do, but *values are things we must do*. Our values come from our base of right and wrong, our belief in God, our sense of morality, our love of things good and hatred of things evil. Our values are things we would fight for, maybe even die for; they are our convictions. Our values determine our purpose in life. In our deep and driving values we find little room for compromise, for to compromise would be to cut away an important piece of ourselves.

We might place values into two categories in order to understand them better. There are motivating values—values regarding money, status, security and comfort; and there are driving values—values concerning justice, honesty, integrity, belief in God. While all of our values are very strong within us, our motivating values can be bent some, not easily, but they can be bent. If you were in a relationship where you discovered differences in your motivating values, you could possibly find some place for compromise. For instance, if you highly value money, you might find room for compromise because your partner offers something of higher value, like love and respect.

On the other hand, it is almost impossible to compromise our driving values, and rightly so. They are deep within us and make up who we are! One of our most important driving values is our faith system, our belief in God. It would be a terrible mistake to compromise our belief in God. I believe the injunction in Scripture against marrying someone outside of the faith is one of Paul's wisest warnings. Imagine, if for the sake of a relationship, you were asked to compromise your honesty, integrity or relationship with God. This is a high price to pay for companionship, a price that doesn't have an adequate return on investment.

One of the functions of the Hoping Stage is to discover just where there are areas of commonality in our interests and values. If we find areas of overlap, we move forward. If we find too few similarities, it is unlikely the relationship will grow. Many times a couple will attempt to proceed in the relationship in spite of vast differences in interests and values. Reality generally sets in at a later date when one or both of the partners find themselves feeling very frustrated and angry about the relationship.

Rapport

The second place that we are searching for areas of overlap is mutual rapport—how we get along, issues of personality. In the third chapter we looked at personality types and how each of us is endowed with our own wonderful peculiarities. Sometimes our peculiarities mesh well with someone else's; other times we discover a war zone. It's true that we can learn to get along with anybody, but when we are developing a relationship that might lead to marriage, we need to weigh heavily our compatibility.

We can be immediately attracted to someone with our same personality type because we sense so much compatibility. There is the feeling that "I've finally found someone who understands me," "we track so well," "we're on the some wavelength." It is powerfully bonding to feel as if you're understood by someone else. But with the wonderful often comes the wicked. The very thing that draws us together can drive us crazy. Two "feelers" can get so deep with each other that they never really relate; they only talk about relating. Two "initiators" can be so adventuresome and spontaneous that they can't keep up with one another. Two "precisionists" can be well structured, but each can be structured in areas the other feels are unimportant. And two "thinkers" can be so analytical and critical of each other that murder may become a logical alternative.

The point is, personality types cannot determine whether or not we will be compatible with someone. There are great relationships in every possible combination of personality types. Personality types only give us an idea of our general tendencies, of what makes us tick (and what ticks us off). We intuitively know when we are compatible with someone. And when intuition fails us, we can always turn to logic by asking questions like: How well do we get along? Are we comfortable with each other most of the time? Do we spend a lot of time fighting (more than 50 percent)? Am I free to be myself with this person? If we are comfortable with this new person, we continue in the relationship; if we are not, the relationship does not grow.

Potential Complement

Within each of us is a drive toward completeness that can be fulfilled in a relationship with someone of the opposite sex. We find a sense of wholeness in the unity of male and female. We have a deep longing to be bonded in a special way that seems to add to our own personness. The drive for this wholeness is so deep it cannot be denied. The drive is natural, healthy, pure and powerful because it is the way we are built. It is the way we are created. My bias is that we are created in the image of God and that the image of God is composed of both male and female. The writer of Genesis says in beautiful ancient poetry,

> Then God said,
> Let us make mankind in our image, according to our
> likeness. . . .
> And so God created mankind in his image,
> In the image of God he created him,
> Male and female he created them.

Our drive for the wholeness found in a relationship with someone of the opposite sex is simply the drive for "Godness" in our lives, an innate drive for creation intent, to experience the fullness of the image of God.

When we are in the initial stages of a relationship (Hoping), we are subconsciously evaluating the other person as a potential complement to us. Are the traits of maleness or femaleness ones that I need in my life? Do I find nurturing (mother/femaleness)? Is there a aura of protection (father/maleness)? Is there strength, tenderness, love, firmness? Does the other person add strengths to my nonstrengths? These qualities are very difficult to evaluate on a logical scale. They are caught in a net composed of intuition, not logic. Logic gives only indications; our gut speaks loudly. The drive for wholeness is a strong agent in the quest for meaningful relationship. If it is felt, the relationship might continue to grow; if it is not felt, then one, or both, of the partners may be frustrated in the relationship.

Affirmation

Study after study continually demonstrates that the most desired reward that employees seek from employers is not financial gain; it is affirmation. The same holds true for relationships. What is it that we are looking for in our quest for commonality, rapport and potential complement? What is the internal need that is driving us to try to find these qualities in another person? It is our quest for affirmation! It is our need to be affirmed for who we are and who we want to be. It is our need to be affirmed for our unique (and needy) personness.

Can you guess what the key determining factor is to whether a relationship will move beyond the Hoping Stage and on to the Scoping Stage? Responsiveness—responsiveness to who I am, what I feel, what I need and what I like. Responsiveness is the heart of affirmation. If you tell someone your greatest accomplishment and they jump for joy, you have indeed found a friend. But if they respond by saying, "Big deal," you're not going to like them a whole lot. One of the major ways we determine our areas of overlap is by the degree of responsiveness we get from each other.

Again a story about my first date with my wife. Let me preface the story by telling you that I am intrigued by philosophy. So I dabble in weird thought. So . . . back to the first date. As we were driving away from the historic arts and crafts fair, I told Pam of one of my aberrant interpretations of a certain biblical passage. I had told this interpretation to only a select few seminary colleagues out of fear of being called a heretical lunatic. When Pam heard my idea, she responded by saying, "Wow! I've never thought of it that way before. Your idea makes sense. That's good stuff." Let me tell you, I knew right then that she was some special woman—and smart, too, if she agreed with me! What happened in that conversation? Pam was responsive to something that was important to me. And she gave me great affirmation; in essence she told me, "You're a pretty smart guy."

We all need affirmation. In the Hoping Stage of a relationship, affirmation is demonstrated by our responsiveness to one another. So important is affirmation that subsequent moves in a new relationship will be determined by how responsive you and your new friend are to one another. Your relationship will grow in proportion to the amount of affirmation you offer.

Dangers in the Stage

In this Hoping Stage we are deciding whether we would like to move on to the next stage of our new relationship. Our decision should be based on sound communication principles (although the principles are often determined intuitively). But sometimes we base our reasoning for growth on faulty bases.

We fall into what can be called the Dangers of the Stage. The four dangers we need be aware of are physical attraction, chemistry, closed list and stargazing.

Physical Attraction

Physical attraction is one of the most wonderful and most dangerous reasons for developing a relationship. Something inbred within us causes us to desire an attractive person. I recently heard of a study that suggests even babies are drawn to attractive people. But there is another side of desiring an attractive partner—insecurity. We want an attractive partner in order to make us look good. This is the sad side because it allows us to use another person, often unwittingly, for our own gratification. Since a relationship can never last on looks alone, someone always gets hurt.

When we attempt to develop a relationship based on looks, we are doomed for failure. Remember, relationship is communication, and if we fail to communicate, we have no relationship. In relationships that are based on physical attraction, the partners are blinded to the obvious. They can't see the reality of the relationship. They can't see if they have commonality, rapport or complement. An important point to remember here is that the longer you have a relationship with someone, the less looks are an issue. In good relationships people actually become more attractive; in poor relationships people become less attractive. Count on it!

Chemistry

Chemistry and fireworks, that's what meaningful relationship is all about. Right? Hardly. I cannot think of two terms that have been more destructive for relationships than chemistry and fireworks. We just love the magical and mystical; we eat up *Love Boat* and all the stuff that goes with it. And we don't realize that in real life underneath the Love Boat is an enemy sub shooting missiles of reality. Glamour fades about

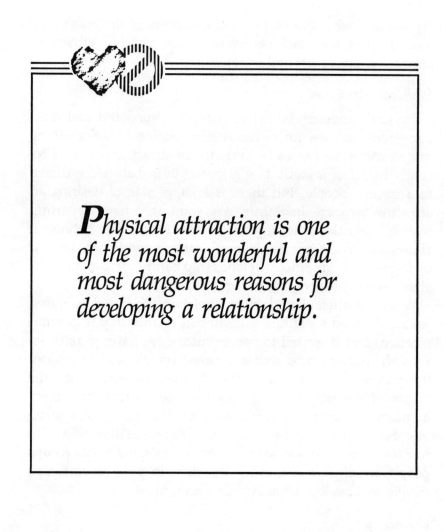

*P*hysical attraction is one
of the most wonderful and
most dangerous reasons for
developing a relationship.

the time your partner says, "Excuse me, but I'm going to get sick all over your front seat." A friend of mine once said that chemistry makes us feel each other's backs for angel's wings when we should be searching each other's heads for horns.

Chemistry makes us even more blind than the obsession with physical attraction because with chemistry we generally receive a double portion of affirmation, acceptance and understanding. It often comes at a point of unusual need, and it's always a surprise. "I would never have imagined that Paul and I could be so close, so deep, so soon!" Part of the wonder is the surprise. Many times it comes in the form of an innocent phone call, and we discover that "we talked all night long." Before we know it, the other person knows our whole life story. We find that we just can't go another minute without seeing him, or at least talking to him. And then comes the downfall—the couple is together all of the time.

Generally, they experience burnout. But, not always. I have seen some successful marriages come from relationships like these. However, more often than not, the relationship ends with two very broken people. So much hope, but much too soon. The infatuation with chemistry is deceiving because the couple is convinced they are having meaningful and intimate communication. They are, but it's much too one-sided; one would never think of doing something that might slightly offend the other. We just can't go through life like that. So, sooner or later, the truth comes out.

Be cautious when you sense that chemistry is attacking you. It can be wonderful, it can be real, but it also can cause much pain. Be careful what color glasses you wear. Chemistry is rose-colored while life is a rainbow, and not all the colors are what you want.

Closed List

In the beginning of the chapter we discussed the idea that we all have a list of characteristics that make up our perfect mate. We cannot deny the reality of our lists, nor should we. Most people don't have their lists written down, but some do. And those are the people I have in mind now.

Are you making your list and checking it twice? If you are, you may be passing up some great prospects for relationship. Some people have a list so tight that only two or three people in the world could fit, and then these people wonder why they are still single. You would be surprised how many people there are with whom you could form meaningful relationships if you would only give them, and yourself, a chance. When I was single (and that was for a long time!), I had a list of things I wanted in a woman, and I found it didn't work. So I tried something new; I did three things. First, I made a very short list of things I wanted in a woman, composed mostly of values. Second, I made a short list of things I didn't want in a woman, things that I absolutely could not live with. These were three or four personality traits. Finally, I left myself open to the possibility of relationship with anybody who fit in that general schema.

I have a friend whose list was so narrow that he was thirty-nine before he married for the first time. He had to change his list considerably or he would have missed the most wonderful woman in the world for him. I'm not suggesting that you might have to settle for second or third best. I'm saying there are a lot of great people that you are passing up by holding too tightly to an unrealistic list.

Stargazing

The danger of stargazing is directly related to the concept of lists. Sometimes our list becomes so strong within us that we develop an imaginary or mythological person, someone among the stars. We are looking for this perfect person to give our life perfection. Now, while this mythological person is floating around in our heads, we meet someone who is kind, affirming, understanding and responsive, and we cry out for joy, "Voila! The woman of my dreams has finally arrived after so many years of hiding!" The danger begins. We immediately slide this new person into the husk of our myth. The new person never gets a chance to be herself; she is now the myth. The obvious danger here is that we are dating a myth, not a real person. So what happens? After a few dates this person begins to act like herself and so starts to crack the myth. And you cry, "You're not the person I thought you were. You're not my star." To which she responds, "No kidding!"

Stargazing explains one reason for repeated promiscuity. A question is often asked of women, "How could a self-respecting woman go to a bar, then go home with a man she doesn't know and get involved sexually?" (I might add that this problem is not at all exclusive to women.) My response is that she is going home and going to bed with someone she knows better than anyone else in the world. She is sleeping with her myth. And then the tragedy strikes. Very quickly she discovers the guy is a jerk and not her myth at all. She is overcome with guilt, remorse and disgust as her heart is broken one more time. Stargazing can hurt you, and your potential partner.

My encouragement regarding all of these dangers: Be realistic! Dream, please dream, but don't let your dreams overwhelm your sense of sanity. Be aware of the basic process of communication and use it to make wise decisions.

What happens next? If you are basing your relationship on reality and if you find enough areas of overlap, then move on to the next stage: scoping out the one.

6

Scoping

Pam and I had been dating for nine weeks. For the first
month we got together only once each week, on Friday
nights. We would eat dinner, chat for a while, and since I
was in my final year of seminary, I would lie around reading
Hebrew while she did something meaningful. For the next
five weeks or so we really got heavy in our relationship and
started seeing each other twice each week—both Friday and
Saturday nights! (I'm kind of a slow mover.) It was the ninth
week of our relationship (I'll never forget it) when I decided it
was time to have one of "those talks." You know what I
mean—one of "those talks" where we have to talk about our
relationship. Up to this point we were both pretending we
didn't have a relationship; it's very safe that way, you know.

Well, the Friday night finally came for our talk. I had it all
rehearsed. I knew exactly what to say. It would be tough, and
she would probably get hurt, but I had to do it. I had to be
honest. I was going to suggest to Pam that, while we were
having a nice time, we should not consider ourselves an
"item." We should be free to date other people if we liked.
We should not take our relationship too seriously.

We had just finished dinner when I said, "Pam, I think it's
time we had one of 'those talks'." To which she responded,
"I'm glad you brought that up. I've been wanting to talk to
you about something. I've been thinking about us, and it
doesn't seem like a good idea for us to get too serious here. I
think we should be free to date other people without any
complications."

I was flabbergasted. How dare she take my line! I mean, I was the one who was supposed to come in with the power play, and she outplayed me. I'll never forget sitting at her dining table feeling as if I were going to die. I was crushed because I realized that what I had indeed really wanted was an exclusive relationship with Pam, but I was just too fearful to admit it.

There I was at her table with my head buried in my Hebrew text when she innocently asked, "Is something wrong?" I then did something I had never done before; I told her what was wrong. I told her I was hurt, and scared because I was hurt. I told her I was confused. And after I was through telling her about my emotions, I felt even worse. Good night, what had I just done? I had let her see my insides, and I felt like such a wimp. I literally felt as if I had just flayed myself and then handed Pam a bottle of rubbing alcohol and said, "What are you going to do with it?" She was wonderful. She was so kind and understanding. She didn't pour alcohol on me. Instead, she sewed my skin back together and said, "I care. And I'm honored that you trusted me with your feelings." I knew then that we had great potential in our relationship because Pam was someone I could trust with my emotions.

The second stage of a relationship is Scoping, scoping out the one. In this stage we begin our major experimentation with openness and vulnerability.

Description of the Stage

The Hoping Stage of a relationship does not generally last a long time. In fact it is usually quite short, spanning three to five meetings, because if the relationship grows at all, it quickly moves on to the next stage. That's because the next stage, Scoping, is where all the action is. In this stage we begin to experiment with meaningful self-disclosure. If the Hoping Stage is characterized by discovery, then the Scoping Stage adds the process of experimentation. While we are delightfully discovering more about our new friend, we are also carefully checking him or her out. How much can I reveal to this other person without getting burned? How close can I safely get?

One of our great desires is to be understood. We all long to have a soul mate who understands and accepts our deep and crazy idiosyncrasies—someone who supports our dreams and desires, who applauds when we win, who cries when we are lonely and scared, and who encourages us when we are frail and weak. We long for the affirmation of just one person who will accept us for who we are and not try to manipulate us into being anyone else, especially someone he or she might want us to be. We all want to be known well . . . and loved anyway; we *need* to be known well and loved anyway.

If we all have the same desires and needs, then what's the problem? Why don't we just get out there and relate openly, honestly and without hesitation? Why don't we simply spill our guts to anyone we meet? We don't do it for one simple reason: we're scared to death! John Powell in his great book on intimacy, *Why Am I Afraid To Tell You Who I Am?*, answers his own question with this, "I am afraid to tell you who I am, because, if I tell you who I am, you may not like who I am, and that's all I have." We don't relate openly, honestly and without hesitation because we are scared to death of rejection.

Two years ago I had a major personal revelation. I discovered something about myself so obvious I was shocked that it took me thirty-six years to see it. My discovery? I am an insecure person. No, I am a very insecure person. And my insecurity has played an instrumental role in the way I have run my life, and my relationships. Along with my own personal revelation I discovered something else: I am not alone. Everyone else is insecure also. We all run around scared to death

We struggle between the driving need to be understood and the paralyzing fear of being known.

of getting hurt, and so we build walls of protection, which become walls of isolation. How did we ever get this way? Let me offer a little parody to show the root of our problem.

"In the beginning" the world was a pretty great place. The man and the woman related to each other openly and honestly; they had a direct hotline to God; and they basically had no fears. It is said that they were "naked and unashamed" (only proving my theory that aerobics were part of the creation plan). But then something happened. The man and the woman discovered avocados. Now God had said they could eat anything in the garden except the avocados. Well, Adam and Eve immediately saw this was unfair. I mean, no avocados meant no guacamole, and that was pushing things just too far. So they ate anyway.

Because they rejected the creation plan, isolation and loneliness were born. They became isolated from each other and from God. Fear and loneliness set in. Then they became aware of their nakedness and began to cover themselves, as we continue to do today. God created us to relate, and the great irony is that what we were created to do is the very thing we are most fearful of doing!

We live our lives in the push-pull struggle of an emotional paradox that keeps us loony. We struggle between the driving need to be understood and the paralyzing fear of being known. We are afraid of being known because if we are truly known, then and only then can we be truly rejected. And if we are truly rejected, we feel as if we have nothing left—no respect, no value, no self-worth, and that's a lot to risk on a relationship. So, too often, we don't risk it.

A heart is a sad thing to waste. For it not to be wasted it must be used, and in order to be used it must be given. But it can't be given if it is paralyzed by fear. Fortunately, however, most of us do not have incurable paralysis. There is hope! The Scoping Stage of a relationship is our antidote for the fearful paralysis. In the Scoping Stage we carefully investigate our partner's trustworthiness, and we experiment with meaningful self-disclosure. The critical groundwork is being laid for the most important element in any relationship—TRUST. Can I trust my deepest feelings with this person? We discover the other person's trustworthiness as we "scope out the one."

Distinctives of the Stage

The goal of open, honest and intimate communication is freedom. We are each striving for the freedom to be real and the freedom to reveal our most cherished secrets to someone who will affirm and respond. We find this freedom through experimentation as we move along the disclosure continuum. The disclosure continuum begins with small talk and safe disclosures, then moves to vulnerable disclosures, and finally culminates in discovered disclosures.

Small Talk

It is popular today to put down small talk. We want to know the bottom line and not waste time with peripheral issues. But surprisingly, small talk is both healthy and wise for a relationship. It is the most common and most comfortable thing we do when we are not well acquainted with someone. And, it is small talk that leads us to deep talk.

When we try to "skip the small talk," we can actually interrupt the route to deep talk. Meaningful communication is built on much more than words alone. The *way* you say something tells a lot about you—your attitudes, convictions and personality. The way you say your words often says much more than the words themselves. (Some experts claim that communication is as much as 85 percent nonverbal.) Small talk can become your ally. Small talk allows you to be yourself and speak comfortably. You don't have to put on as many social pretenses, and you have an opportunity to be real.

Small talk also helps you and your new friend uncover subjects of common interest. In the middle of a seemingly trivial conversation, you can accidentally come upon an area of mutual interest. The talk at that point becomes much less small because you have discovered a subject you both know and love. You can then become deeply involved in a conversation about that subject. After you have explored the area of common interest for a while, you move back into small talk until once again you discover an area of common interest.

Safe Disclosures

As the small talk deepens, so does the quality of your communication. It's exciting to discover new things about each other, especially if that discovery appears to be somewhat personal. But you must be careful here. You need to enter the arena of self-disclosure slowly and deliberately. Experiment to find out just how much personal knowledge you can trust your new friend with. This is done through safe disclosures.

Safe disclosures are items you might not want everybody in the world to know, but you wouldn't die if somebody else found out about them. The subject matter of the safe disclosures varies from person to person. They can be items like a painful breakup in the past, a divorce, a broken dream, a secret passion, an opinion about something. They are personal matters, but they are not critically personal. So you offer a "safe disclosure" to your new friend to see what will be done with it. Will he laugh, smirk, be appalled, gossip? Or will he respond affirmingly and keep the information to himself?

The purpose of safe disclosures is monumental. Without them you could never be sure about the trustworthiness of your new friend. What you are looking for is someone to trust, someone who will affirm you and who will not gossip about you. Test the trustworthiness of your new friend by experimenting with these safe disclosures. Evaluate carefully how your new friend received your safe disclosure. If he passed the test, send out another one; if he failed, be very careful. Proceed wisely. You know the old saying, "Burn me once, shame on you; burn me twice, shame on me."

Vulnerable Disclosures

After you have entrusted your new friend with several safe disclosures, and he has responded with affirmation and trustworthiness, you then can begin meaningful self-disclosure. You can begin to talk about yourself and issues of life without fear of being deeply hurt by your friend's response. This is the heart of communication and meaningful relationship. This is where you really develop your relationship and risk being truly known. The bonding that takes place when you are free to talk openly, honestly and without hesitation is unparalleled. You develop the freedom to be insecure.

I have a friend who is a nationally known author and lecturer. As we were first getting to know each other, we used to sit and talk for hours at a hamburger stand that overlooked a lake. One day, while sipping a chocolate malt, I discovered something about my new friend. He, too, was an insecure man. He was popular, had made a name for himself, and yet, he was insecure. But more importantly, he gave me the freedom to be insecure also. Our relationship held the possibility of depth. Because of the freedom to be insecure we now have a relationship that is continually growing and bonding.

What kind of information falls into the category of vulnerable disclosures? I think we get a little mixed up here. We often think we are being vulnerable when we pull our dirty clothes from the laundry, when we tell someone about our most embarrassing moment, or reveal some deep dark secret out of our past. Our dark past actually has little to do with vulnerability. What happens when we have told all of our dirty little stories? Does that mean we have nothing intimate left to share? Or do we have to wait for another major foul-up? Absolutely not! *The heart of vulnerability is discovered in the present, not in the past.* The heart of vulnerability is how you feel now, what you think now, who you are now, not yesterday. Vulnerability is saying to a friend, "You know, I'm afraid my boss doesn't like me, and I hate not being liked," or "I know this might sound stupid, but I get jealous when I see you talking to Bill," or "I really like Barry Manilow." (Now that's really being vulnerable, and you guessed it—I love Barry Manilow.)

Being vulnerable is having the freedom to reveal your heart, your fears, your self-concept, your real desires, your failures, and your successes. (Most of us don't have the forum we need to brag on ourselves.) The freedom to be vulnerable is vital to the success of a meaningful relationship; it's what relationship is all about. But it takes time, testing, experimenting and discovery. It takes a process.

Discovered Disclosures

This final aspect of the disclosure continuum can be experienced only after you have successfully passed through the first three. Discovered disclosures come only with the most intimate of relationships. They are discovery of character traits that were not known even to you until the development of this new relationship. The intimacy of your relationship can grow so deep that you discover things about yourself. And you have the forum to discuss this new revelation. My discovery of my own insecurity was the direct result of the intimacy developed in my marriage.

There is a proverb that says, "One person sharpens another as iron sharpens iron." The idea is that two hearts go deeper than one, two minds know more than one, two spirits are wiser than one. Such is an intimate relationship based on open and honest communication.

Who's Afraid?

Who has a more difficult time with vulnerability, men or women? Who has a harder time sharing their feelings, men or women?

Men, in general, have a harder time sharing their emotions. In fact, men generally have a harder time understanding their emotions than women do. Women are just freer about these things. Think about it. Women don't need a reason to get together; they can get together simply to talk. Illustration of a phone call. Jane's phone rings:

Jane: Hello.

Mary: Hi, Jane. This is Mary.

Jane: Hi, Mary. What's going on with you?

Mary: Nothing really. I just called to talk.

Jane: Oh great, did you hear . . .

Now, let's take the same scenario with Fred and Phil. Fred's phone rings:

Fred: Yo.

Phil: Hey, Fred. Phil here.

Fred: Hi there. What d'ya want?

Phil: Oh nothin' really. I just called to talk.

Fred: (silence) Uh . . . about what?

Phil: Nothing. I just thought we could talk.

Fred: What's wrong? You got girl troubles? What's up?

Phil: No, Fred. I just wanted to talk.

Fred: (silence) Hey, are you taking drugs again?

Men need a reason to get together. They don't just get together to talk; they have to be doing something, like playing cards, going to a ballgame, working on a project, or having the famous gossip session disguised as a committee meeting. Women don't have to play this stuff. They can call it like it is—let's just get together and talk. Part of the problem is cultural. I heard once that men are raised with two notions: to stay cool (don't show emotion) and to rule (get ahead). The preoccupation with antiemotionalism has led to the humorous machismo attitude, the macho man. But the macho man is dying on the inside because he doesn't know how to do what he was created to do: to relate.

Women are the much wiser sex in this regard. I believe it is more than just cultural. Women seem to be more emotionally gifted and are more natural at self-disclosure. They learn early the importance of honest self-disclosure. But something happens later in life. They get burned once, twice, a third and a fourth time until they, too, become closed and afraid. The truth of the matter is that we all have a fear of intimacy, and all of us must begin the process of breaking out of it.

Commitment and Trust

What is the process of breaking out of that fear? It is a matter of finding someone we can trust. The Scoping Stage might be defined as the process of developing trust. As we move along the disclosure continuum from small talk to vulnerable disclosure, we are developing trust in our new friend. We are determining whether or not we can reveal our heart to him or her. Lewis Smedes, an author, lecturer and professor at Fuller Seminary, has said we are most like God when we keep our promises. We are forever searching for that godlike quality in other people, that quality that will be true and faithful. When we arrive at the level of vulnerable disclosure, we have found a friend we can trust.

Here you find the first signs of commitment. Commitment sneaks up on you. When you have the freedom to disclose vulnerable information to someone, you have already experienced commitment. You see, we view commitment from strictly an obligatory point of view, when actually there are two sides of commitment: obligation and emotion. Commitment usually begins with emotional commitment. Two people are committed to caring for each other emotionally. Emotional commitment is what it takes to be vulnerably open. You would never reveal your heart to someone unless you felt reasonably certain he or she was committed to doing good things with the information. I am not speaking about a formal agreement. The commitment has been made implicitly. It is a tacit commitment, but it is very real. And it is the route to the deeper commitment we will discuss in the Coping Stage and in the third section of the book.

A Wisdom Approach

We must be careful as we grant greater trust; we don't want to give our heart to someone who will throw it on the ground and step on it. As you go through the disclosure continuum, use some wisdom. Don't set yourself up for the emotional kill. I have three suggestions. The first two are for the giver (the one who is disclosing), and the third one is for the receiver (the one being told).

1. *Be Selective.* Be selective of the person with whom you are seeking to communicate intimately. Is this a trustworthy person? What has he done with the information you have given him thus far? Has he affirmed or laughed or been appalled or been critical and cruel? Don't give anyone any more than he has earned the right to know!

2. *Be Discerning.* Be discerning of where you are in the stages of your relationship and on the disclosure continuum. Don't be vulnerable until you have been safe. Don't get too deep too quickly. We will look more at that in a minute.

3. *Be Responsible.* Be responsible when someone else chooses to reveal vulnerable information to you. Remember, you are being chosen to receive a great privilege—another person's heart. There are two common errors you must avoid: (1) Don't be "shocked" when someone reveals something shocking. Don't say, "I don't believe you could have done that!" (2) Don't tell! The worst thing in the world we can ever do is to reveal a given secret. Our honor is damaged while another person's heart is broken.

Dangers in the Stage

Some of us are old pros at getting deep with another person; others of us seem to have a tough time doing it well. All of us, however, fall into traps that can block further development of intimate communication. If we are at least aware of some of the dangers, we may be able to prevent their damaging our prospective relationships. Let's look at some of the dangers in the Scoping Stage of a relationship.

Too Much Too Soon

Some personality types have the ability to get deep very quickly. In fact, they seem to thrive on it. But an inherent danger in getting too deep too soon is giving too much information too soon. People are just not ready for all our goods in one package, especially when the package includes a lot of negative baggage. In its early stages a relationship is very brittle and can be broken easily. If we offer some personal and shameful information to a new friend, it is difficult for that person to process the information well. Remember, he doesn't have a whole lot of good stuff to compensate for the bad stuff. So he naturally begins to wonder, "Just who is this person anyway?"

Years ago when I was in business, I met a woman through some business affiliations. As we ran into each other frequently, we discovered many "areas of overlap," not the least of which was that I found her attractive. So a "date" seemed to be the natural next step. I had her over for dinner one night. After a great meal (I used to be a good cook), we sat down to chat. As our conversation became more revealing, she told me she had twice been extremely violent, that she had even stabbed a person once. Let me tell you, I needed to hear no more. "So long, amiga, I'm outta here!" I never dated her again!

Possibly there was a good reason for her behavior. Self-defense? Who knows? But I was not staying around long enough to find out. Why? Because I did not have enough good data to counter the negative data. Revealing too much too soon can be very damaging to the relationship.

Too Deep Too Long

This problem piggybacks off of the first one. It, too, is a pitfall of those personalities who have the ability to get very deep very quickly. Some people are almost obsessed with the desire for meaning and depth. They have utter distaste for small talk, trivia and silliness. Everything must be deep. And so, they can wring the life out of their partner, or out of each other. They stay up until the wee hours of the morning talking deeply. They are constantly evaluating their relationship, discussing how well they talk, analyzing themselves and the other's personality and motivation.

I counsel a lot of people who fall into this trap. Somewhere along the line they find themselves absolutely drained of energy. I once counseled a couple like this who spent so much time analyzing their relationship that they had forgotten how to relate! All they could do was talk about it; they couldn't do it. My advice was for them to go to the beach, walk hand in hand, watch the sunset and evaluate nothing. They were not to talk about what a good time they were having, just have a good time. (They broke up two weeks later.)

Men and Machismo

A common roadblock to intimate communication is the difficulty some men have in relating openly and honestly. Remember, men are raised with the notions to be cool and to rule. Spilling your guts hardly fits into the "be cool" category. The sad thing is that many men might like to be more open and honest but simply don't know where to start. They don't even know how to access those emotions. I am convinced, however, that with a sensitive partner and with an awareness of the disclosure continuum, these men, too, can develop meaningful, intimate communication.

But there is another side. Some men think they should never relate or communicate in the ways we have discussed in this chapter. They believe they are above such a thing. Those people are cutting themselves off from one of the greatest joys in life—intimate communication. Don't allow a mistaken attitude to prevent you from attaining what you really desire—love.

Women's Expectations of Men

One brief word of caution: women, don't expect men to relate as you do! Men and women are different. Scientific evidence proves it! Men not only look different from women, they also behave differently, and they relate differently. A man does not see the world through the same glasses as a woman. He responds differently. So, women, don't think that a man isn't sensitive just because his sensitivity might be shown in strange ways. Take the time to talk about it and find out what he thinks and feels.

Sex

The astute reader will have noticed a marked absence in the text thus far. Sex has not been discussed. Does that mean I don't like sex? No, I think sex is great. As a matter of fact, I think sex is dynamite. The problem is, sometimes it can blow up a relationship.

Part of the problem is that we have greatly confused sex and intimacy in the relational world today. Sex and intimacy are not the same things. Sex is only one aspect of intimacy; intimacy is much greater than intercourse. Don't get me wrong. Sex is a very intimate encounter, one of the most intimate we can ever experience. But *sex is not the basis for intimacy; it is the fruit of intimacy*. Sex cannot be the foundation for our relationship. It is, rather, the culmination of our relationship. That's why I believe sexual intercourse should be limited to one partner, the partner of a lifelong commitment in marriage.

Sex was designed "from the beginning" for pleasure, for procreation and for unique union. The threefold purpose of sex is like a package. You can't have one without the others. Sex in a dating relationship only focuses on one of the purposes, namely pleasure. But what about the other two? Obviously, procreation is not desirable in a dating relationship. But we can't help being somehow mystically bonded by the sex act. And our relationship is not ready for that mystical bond, especially when the bond was intended by God for permanence. I think that is what Paul is driving at in 1 Corinthians 6.

Sexual activity in the early stages of a relationship can be destructive because it gives a false sense of closeness. If a couple has been "naked and unashamed" in a physical sense, an emotional sense of security and intimacy follows. But the intimacy is based on nothing substantial. When my wife and I were dating, she brought up an excellent point about sex. If a couple is involved sexually, they spend much of their quality time together either having sex or thinking about it. If they have developed the habit of "fooling around" at the end of the date, then during the earlier hours of the date they find themselves anxiously awaiting eleven o'clock so they can get to the "good stuff." It so preoccupies their minds that it destroys the possibility of meaningful communication. Ironically, they rob themselves of the joy of lasting intimacy for the sake of immediate physical intimacy.

I am not here to tell you what to do or what not to do. There are plenty of others in my profession who are much better suited for that than I. What I am here to do is to beg you, be wise! Know what you're getting yourself into. Sex isn't all it's cracked up to be when you give your most prized possession (your body) and have it rejected by your partner deciding to find someone else. Sex isn't all it's cracked up to be when it, ironically, robs you of the real intimacy you are seeking. Sex, out of proper timing, can be counterproductive to your relationship. You know, God's plans are not so crazy after all!

If you are at this Scoping Stage, now is a great time to evaluate your relationship before going on to the next stage of Coping. Coping is the stage where you will begin the real work of commitment. You start to view yourselves as a twosome, no longer as solos. Is your relationship ready for that? Are you communicating intimately? If so, then move on. If not, go back and work on the important basics of disclosure.

7

Coping

About three months into our dating, Pam and I had another crisis, again revolving around the issue of how seriously we were taking our relationship. One of her male friends from church had come upon two tickets for the symphony and asked Pam if she would like to join him.

Now, before getting into the crisis, let me regress a bit. About two weeks before this, Pam and I had decided not to be "exclusive." And we had only just begun to "go public" with our relationship. For more than two months very few people even knew we were dating. So only two weeks after we had decided not to be exclusive, here comes this guy asking her to go to the symphony. (She didn't even like the symphony until she met me!) Anyway, Pam felt that she was obliged to accompany this bozo to the Oregon Symphony (which, by the way, is a superb symphony).

Needless to say, I didn't like this situation one bit. Even if he was "only a friend" and there was "nothing romantic between them," I still didn't like it. I quickly realized that what I needed was an exclusive relationship. But I had typical mixed feelings about the deal. I wanted the freedom not to be tied down, I wanted to be able to date someone else if I pleased, but I didn't want her to have the same freedom. So we did it again. We had one of "those talks."

We decided that *if we wanted our relationship to work, we were going to have to work on our relationship.* First, we decided to call it a relationship. We admitted that we liked each other enough to pursue something more lasting. Next, we chose to be exclusive, and by moving in the same direction we could better see the future (if any) in our relationship. We realized that we would have to learn to cope with each other and with our relationship.

The next stage of a relationship is Coping. It is here that more meaningful bonds are formed and deeper trust is realized as we increase our level of commitment.

Description of the Stage

It is difficult to say how long each stage of a relationship should last before moving on to the next stage. Sometimes the Scoping Stage can last only one month before moving to the Coping Stage; other times it can carry on for several months. I believe, however, that the Scoping Stage will normally span a period of one to four months.

It is important to note here that just because you are moving on to a subsequent stage in your relationship, that doesn't mean you stop doing what got you this far in the first place. You must continue to communicate openly and intimately; continue to be vulnerable; continue to develop emotional trust. What happens now is that you add more responsibilities to your relationship.

The Coping Stage of a relationship begins the serious movement to being a couple. In fact, some communicators even call this stage "coupling," referring to it as the time when a couple develops an attitude of "we-ness." In this stage the two romantic friends truly view themselves as a couple, thereby relinquishing some of their rights of independence and starting the wonder of interdependence. Here other people also begin to view them as a couple.

How does this happen? *The key to the Coping Stage is commitment*—commitment to each other and to the relationship. This commitment is demonstrated by increased emotional concern, by more clearly understood expectations and by a mutual understanding of the direction of the relationship.

Coping is the final stage before a couple decides to make a lifelong commitment to the relationship; therefore, it is a critical stage. It is the final test of trustworthiness. You will determine whether you want to trust your very life to this person. That is why it is essential to test your partner's ability to make and keep commitments. Can you trust your partner to do and say what he commits to? That is the function of this penultimate stage of a relationship, coping with the one.

Distinctives of the Stage

Exclusivity

I learned something from my nineteen years of dating. *It is impossible to work on more than one dating relationship at a time.* Do I mean you should never date more than one person at a time? No, and yes. If by "date" you mean a very casual relationship that is still in the Hoping Stage or very early in the Scoping Stage, I see nothing wrong with dating more than one person. But if by "dating" you mean getting serious about more than one relationship, then I emphatically say, "No way, José!"

After your relationship is well into the Scoping Stage, it is impossible for you and your partner to grow any closer unless you are dating exclusively. To try to be serious about more than one person at a time is a contradiction in terms. After all, one of the key qualities you are trying to develop is trust. Emotional trust is the mainstay of the Scoping Stage where you ask the question, "Can I trust this person with my deepest feelings?" How can you trust someone if you are concerned about his or her commitment to you as a valuable person? How can you be trusted if you have conflicts of romantic interests?

Remember, this is the stage of coupling, where the two are

viewing themselves as one, as a unit. There is no room for triads. By the time a relationship has evolved to the Coping Stage, it is unquestionable that it must be exclusive.

We need desperately in our day to return to the joy of monogamy. We were created to live and die with one partner, to share the good and the bad, to be there for each other when no one else will be. We need to be known well and loved anyway, and that can only happen when we are exclusive and monogamous, even in our dating relationships! There is no other way that you can fairly evaluate your relationship.

Coupling

The process of becoming a couple is one that starts the day two people first meet. It continues with your first date and goes on through the Hoping and Scoping Stages. When you reach the Coping Stage, you don't suddenly say, "Let's be a couple." Rather, you discover that you have been becoming a couple all along, that you are indeed already a couple. And you have noticed that your friends are treating you as a couple.

A precious part of the coupling process is establishing your own "personal history." Over the weeks and months you have been dating, you have been collecting numerous shared experiences. You have been developing your own personal history, a history that is unique to your relationship. It belongs only to you; no one else can really appreciate it, nor should they. This personal history of shared experiences is incredibly bonding. Little things become the delicacies of your relationship: songs, restaurants, places enjoyed together (a particular place on the beach or by a lake), memories of special times (often mundane when they first occurred, but the memory of which has become delightfully charming). You find these little delicacies to have a certain magic to them as they become grounds for deeper affection.

Along with the personal history comes the discovery of each other's inner personness: idiosyncrasies, habits, likes, dislikes, passions. Each of you has learned to respond to the other's inner self in a way that only a lover can.

Pam seems to know my inner self better than I do. Let me give you an example. We visited her family in Pittsburgh one Christmas. While we were eating Christmas dinner, one of my in-laws asked if I liked a certain food. I couldn't remember ever trying it. So I asked Pam, "Honey, do I like that?" Everybody at the table got a kick out of a guy who has to ask his wife what he likes. The point is that we have developed such a shared personal history that we know each other extremely well. Such is the case with coupling; it is a powerful tool for bonding the relationship.

Commitment

In the Scoping Stage the commitment we are looking for is an emotional one. We want to know that our new friend is committed to us emotionally. And as that commitment is shown, greater trust develops. But the greatest trust comes from kept promises. Here in the Coping Stage we see the work of "I promise."

Commitment is a two-sided coin. On one side there is the emotional commitment. On the other side there is the equally powerful contractual commitment. It is the side whose "word is as good as gold." It is the side that is quite unpopular today in our "what's in it for me" culture. However, without it we cannot develop the trust we are all looking for. Contractual commitment says, "I will" and does. Commitment is incomplete without both sides of the coin. It is unbalanced if it is only emotional, or if it is purely contractual. A chart will help to visualize the differences.

*T*he greatest trust comes
from kept promises.

Contractual Commitment	Emotional Commitment
Compelled	Impelled
Contractual	Emotional
Responsible	Responsive
Task oriented	Feelings oriented

We all warm to the idea of emotional commitment because it suggests that people love us because their hearts move them to do so. We want people to love us because they really like us, because we are wonderful, because we deserve it. But what about the times we don't deserve it? Or, what about the times our partner just decides to go flaky on us? Or, what about the times we just don't feel like feeling like it? The truth of life is that we are not always motivated by the purest of motivations. The truth of life is that we all have the enormous capacity to be pretty flaky. For this reason we desperately need contractual commitment. We are dying for someone, just one someone, who will keep his or her word to us—someone to count on, someone to trust.

In the Coping Stage of your relationship you must begin to exercise more of the contractual commitment. You need to begin making promises that you must keep because you are establishing habits for the future. If you establish the habit of keeping promises, you are likely to keep those promises should the relationship lead to marriage; if either of you establishes the habit of breaking promises . . . look out!

What kinds of contractual promises can you make during the Coping Stage of the relationship? Here are four promises commonly made in this stage.

1. *Emotional Commitment:* The commitment to emotional concern that has been developing through the Scoping Stage needs to continue and increase. Remember, both sides of the

commitment coin are invaluable. Verbalize your emotional commitment. Leave nothing for assumption.

2. *Exclusivity:* The commitment to exclusivity should not be assumed or just understood. It should be stated and agreed upon. Unstated agreements are dangerous because most often one person is expecting the other person to do something he or she never agreed to do. A mutual agreement to exclusivity gives you a means to test your faithfulness and your partner's faithfulness. Without faithfulness, trust is impossible.

3. *Everyday Issues:* Commitments in everyday issues, over a period of time, reveal important attitudes about trustworthiness. Take Rob and Barb. Two weeks before a wedding, Rob says, "Oh sure Barb, I'll go to Terri's wedding with you. Count on it!" But the day before the wedding, "I'm sorry Barb. How did I know the Rams would make the playoffs and I would get a ticket to the game." Everyday issues are those little promises we make all the time but think little of their immediate importance, and yet, these everyday issues tell on us. Are we faithful or flaky?

4. *Engagement:* An important commitment in this stage is to a mutually understood direction in the relationship. Where are we going anyway? This often comes in an engagement to be married. Or, it can be a commitment to consider engagement, kind of a pre-engagement. As a matter of fact, I do a lot of pre-engagement counseling in which a couple comes to explore the possibility of marriage. I love pre-engagement counseling; I think it's a great idea. A couple comes to me and says, "We're not sure where our relationship is heading. We're ready to consider the possibility of marriage, but we're not ready for marriage." In other words, we want our relationship to go somewhere; we're ready to call it love or call it quits. That is an important commitment in the Coping Stage of a relationship.

Mutual Respect

In this stage we are indeed learning to cope with one another as a couple. We are learning to be just a little less independent and a little more interdependent. We are managing to accept the other person's downsides, the personality quirks. We are learning to share ourselves, to make and keep commitments. Critical to this coping process is the confidence that our partner thinks we are worthy and valuable people, that our partner respects us. One of the worst things we can do to our relationship is shoot one another with verbal potshots.

If one of the partners senses a lack of respect from the other, the whole process shuts down. A relationship is built on the invaluable self-worth of each of the individuals. This is vitally important in a day when both sexes are being recognized as equally significant contributors to the economy and administration of the household. Nothing can destroy a relationship faster than people feeling as if they are being taken advantage of, or that their opinion no longer counts.

Dangers in the Stage

At least three dangers can occur in the Coping Stage. The dangers come from curious friends, broken trust and the battle of independence versus interdependence.

Curious Friends

Each of us lives in at least one subculture. Subcultures are made up of the various groups with which we associate, such as job associates, friends, political groups, community groups, church groups. We commonly find our dating partners from these subgroups. These groups have a nasty habit. They love to talk about the people who are dating within them. The couple becomes an "item." The danger lies in the questions asked of the couple. "Betty, are you still dating Jim? How is it going?"

Questions asked of a couple place too much pressure on a relationship that, at its early stages, can withstand very little pressure. After only two or three dates, two people are a long way from being a couple. But their friends won't let them think so. The innocent and well-intentioned questions of friends can often destroy a relationship before it even begins. I have seen the worst of this in church singles groups.

My advice is threefold. First, to the dating couple: Keep it as quiet as you can; don't make a big deal out of one date. It will fly back at you in the long run. Second, to their friends: Back off! You don't realize it, but your talking about a relationship can actually damage a good thing. Third, to everyone: Use wisdom; try to be aware of how your words affect others.

Broken Trust

Let's admit one fact: we are very scared of relationships. We are scared of being hurt, of being taken advantage of, of being lied to. We break out of our fears only when we are able to count on our partner's trustworthiness. That is why it is essential for us to make a conscious effort to be as honest and trustworthy as possible.

I am going to be vulnerable and share something very personal with you, not because I am an exhibitionist nor because it is easy for me, but because I think it will help make an important point. I wrote a poem to Pam the day before Valentine's Day. I was feeling especially stressful because the following day I was going to speak to more than four thousand people. My fears of speaking drew me deep within myself, and I wrote this poem.

Valentine's Reflection

I am fearful, my love — public speaking does that to
    me . . .
    It is a symbolic reminder of how fearful I am of
      life:
      of failure
      of people and their opinions
      of not being as good as another
      of not doing what I want to do
      of not doing what I *must* do
      of not knowing what I want to do
      of not knowing what I *must* do
      of letting people down
      of not caring enough
      of being too cold and callous
      of people wanting a piece of me
      of people not wanting a piece of me
      of people rejecting me
      of me.
BUT I AM NOT AFRAID OF YOU.
    Your love is true and honest and from your heart.
    I am not afraid of you, and I wonder if you know
      what that means:
        it is maybe the essence of love;
        it is miraculous;
        it is sacramental.
    You are grace, and together we share the deepest
      part of God.

"I am not afraid of you." Are there any more wonderful
words to be able to say to someone? What if we were to con-

sciously and continually build our partner's trust in us? Can you imagine how strong our relationships would be?

Don't play games behind your partner's back. I believe that is part and parcel to adultery. The commandment in the Bible about not committing adultery is less interested in sex than it is in promise keeping. Adultery is only the consequence of a much greater problem. When Jesus talks about adultery in the fifth chapter of Matthew, he says, "If you even think about it, you've done it." What Jesus is interested in is our hearts. Are we faithful and trustworthy? Remember, we are most like God when we keep our promises. Our God is a "covenant-keeping God," so we also should be covenant-keeping people.

If trust is broken in a relationship, is it possible to restore it? Absolutely! But not easily. After trust has been broken, it must once again be earned by renewed and continued fidelity to the promise. The ease of reconciliation depends on the severity of the trust broken. That is why it is so important that we try our best to be faithful, trustworthy people.

Independence vs. Interdependence

Part of coupling is winning the battle of independence and interdependence. People who have been single for a long time have generally developed very independent life-styles in order to survive. "No one is going to provide for me. So if I'm going to survive, I must do it myself." The independent life-style can become so ingrained that it is difficult to let go, and yet, let go we must if we are to have a meaningful relationship.

The move to interdependence is important in the Coping Stage and essential for the survival of your relationship. In order to be a couple, we must pare down certain rights of independence. We are no longer in a position to do "what we want when we want." There is another very important person to consider. The move to interdependence is witnessed most clearly by the way we make decisions. Are we getting the other person's input, even on strictly personal matters? If we are truly becoming a couple, we must truly think and act as one. And when decisions are made that concern both parties, both parties must be a part of the decision-making process. That's one of the reasons we become a couple—to complement one another. We must risk interdependence if we want to move toward intimacy.

If you have made it through the Coping Stage, then "you've come a long way baby!" But what next? The next move is certainly the scariest because it is a lifelong commitment; it is marriage. Now that you have come this far, how do you know for sure if you should get married? Should you call it love (get married), or call it quits (get outta Dodge)? The following chapter, Roping, will help you decide that eternally difficult question.

8

Roping

The continuing saga of Pam and Charlie . . . The day finally came when I decided to ask Pam to marry me. I doubt that a woman could ever know how enormously difficult that is for a man. First, he has to determine that it is the right thing to do. Does he really want to get married—and to her? Then, after weeks (and months) of lost sleep trying to make the decision to ask her, he has to ask her. And she could say no! How could she say no? Doesn't she know what he has gone through? Well, Pam didn't say no. In fact, she responded with the treasured words, "Of course I will!"

A month or so later we were reminiscing about the night of our engagement, and somehow the subject came up of why she said yes to my proposal. The answer was clear and simple, "I couldn't think of any reason not to." That might sound like a cold, nonfeeling reason to get married, but I think it was a wonderful reason; in fact, I was honored to hear it. I had no doubt of her tender, loving feelings toward me. What she added by her comment was that she saw no serious weak spots in our relationship. There were no areas that she felt needed major surgery. We had gone through the stages of a relationship well, and we had every reason to anticipate that we would go through the stages of marriage well.

The Roping Stage is the final stage of a relationship where the couple makes a public declaration of their lifelong commitment to mutual care and fidelity—to marriage. How do you make a decision of such monstrous proportions? How do you know when you should call it love or call it quits?

Marriage is the inseparable union of two very selfish and self-centered people who, in order to survive, must learn to be less selfish and less self-centered.

Description of the Stage

Tim Timmons opens all of his wedding ceremonies humorously with the statement, "Weddings are a time of great joy; it's the living together afterward that causes all the trouble." We laugh, but we also shiver because that statement rings so true. We're scared of marriage. We're afraid of failure, of being married to the wrong person and of becoming another tragic divorce statistic. And so we search for the right partner with great care, with fear and trembling. But I wonder if sometimes we search too hard, looking for too much.

I believe that in the midst of so much literature and preaching on marriage, we have become dazed and confused about it. Marriage is quite simple, you know. We complicate it by expecting it to be the "be all and end all" of life. We expect our marriage to provide for our personal fulfillment in life. But I don't think that is the purpose of marriage. Marriage is an economic institution provided by God for the survival and welfare of his people. It is more for survival than for fulfillment. Through marriage we contribute to the needs of our partner, we receive help from our partner and we expand God's kingdom on earth.

Marriage is a loving sacrifice. And if both parties are prepared to sacrifice for each other, a marriage will be amazingly rewarding. My definition of marriage is that "Marriage is the inseparable union of two very selfish and self-centered people who, in order to survive, must learn to be less selfish and less self-centered."

The survival of a marriage is directly related to each partner's willingness to consider the other's needs. We are all very needy people. We need love, acceptance and care. But in order to receive them, we must also give them, and that means letting go of some of our ego. Herein lies the wonder of marriage: two people learning to think less of themselves and more of the other person, two people learning to forgive and be forgiven, to reconcile their differences, to love simply because they choose to do so—two people learning to be more like our God.

If marriage is learning to be less selfish and self-centered, then the stages of a relationship form the process by which we become less selfish and more other-centered. In the Hoping Stage we were quite selfish, asking how this other person fits us. In the Scoping Stage we were becoming less selfish as we were caring for the emotional needs of our new friend. In the Coping Stage we became much less selfish because we were making sacrificial commitments to the other person. And in the Roping Stage we must become very other-centered as we promise to care for our mate for the rest of his or her life.

Distinctives of the Stage

The commitment to the lifelong experience of marriage is certainly one of the most important decisions we will ever make. Therefore, our decision must be made with wisdom and insight. How do you wisely evaluate whether your relationship is ready for marriage? If you have successfully passed through the previous stages, you are likely a candidate for marriage. By means of quick review, let's use what we have learned in the previous stages. Let's look at four thermometers that can take the temperature of your relationship: hoping and commonality, scoping and communication, coping and commitment, and trust.

Hoping and Commonality

The thermometer of commonality includes all of the items we discussed in the Hoping Stage: interests, values, rapport and complement. How well do your interests merge? Do you enjoy similar kinds of recreation, hobbies, avocations? If not, would you mind doing some of these things with your partner? Would you protest if your partner did some of these things alone? Most importantly, have you discussed how you will manage potential conflicts of interest? Even though Pam and I had some very different interests, we have learned to enjoy many of them together (except shopping, but I've gotten better).

The key area of commonality is your values. Do you have any major differences about religion, ethics/morality, perhaps even politics? If so, how severe is the sacrifice you would have to make? How much of a sacrifice would you ask your partner to make? You will not be able to compromise your values for very long. And when it comes to your values regarding God, compromise could be devastating. Don't assume that your partner will change. *One of the worst mistakes you could ever make is to assume that your partner will change after you are married.* If you have common values, you have an asset in your relationship. If not, be very careful and know what you are getting yourself into. You could be heading for big trouble.

By this point in your relationship you have discovered those little quirks in your partner's personality that just drive you up a wall. Maybe the quirks surface rarely, but they do exist. How do you handle them? Have you ever discussed them? Most of the time it can be worked out, but it must be worked on in order to be worked out. Are you doing that? What about your good areas of rapport? Don't forget to consider the places that your personalities merge well.

If two people have little in common, it is unlikely that the relationship will progress to the Roping Stage; they usually will break up before that point. However, I have had a few couples in premarital counseling whose differences were so great that I was amazed they had come that far. Their differences put unusual strain on the relationship.

The basic question to be asked here is, "Can I live with this person?" "Do we have enough in common?" Or, "Are we so different that we will drive each other crazy?"

Scoping and Communication

Remember, relationship is communication. It is the basis upon which the relationship stands. In order to have any hope at all for a successful marriage, a relationship must have good communication at its heart. The question to ask is do you have the freedom to be real?

There are two sides of the freedom issue to consider. The first regards your own freedom. Do you have the freedom to act and say what is truly on your heart? Do you have the freedom to share the secrets of your heart? Have you found your partner to be kind, interested and affirming? Have you been trying to break your own personal barriers of insecurity? If so, you have a potentially great relationship. The second issue of freedom concerns your partner. Does he or she open up to you? Is there a wall or barrier?

The quality of your communication can be measured by three criteria: (1) The kind of topics you discuss. Are they meaningful issues, or are they always superficial? (2) The depth of the topics you discuss. Do you go deeper than the surface? (3) The degree of disclosure that takes place. Are you vulnerable with one another? Or, are you afraid of each other because you have developed some hurtful habits of communication?

A great relationship is like a safe harbor. When you are out at sea (in society, business, daily duties), your ship has to be tight. The sails must be trimmed, the hull clean and the guns ready for war. But in your home or in your relationship, you must be in a safe harbor with an ally, not an enemy. You have to be able to let your sails down. They may even be ripped. You might have barnacles underneath, and your guns may be rusty. Your safe harbor is where you talk about the joys and trials of life, where you communicate your soul to your greatest ally.

Communication is the basis for commitment and commonality because it allows the issues to be laid out on the table and cleaned up. Are you free to be you in this relationship? Does your partner feel the freedom to be real? Evaluate this well, and then TALK ABOUT IT!

Coping and Commitment

In the Scoping Stage your relationship was evaluated largely on the basis of emotional response. You experienced a wonderful time of discovery and acceptance. You learned the pleasures of loving someone. But what about when the going gets tough? What about when you no longer *feel* like working on your relationship? What about when the fireworks barely flicker? It happens to all relationships, you know. What then? Do you throw in the towel, or do you dig in and go to work? This is where you evaluate your willingness to cope with your partner, and his or her willingness to cope with you.

Coping comes by committing on both an emotional and a contractual level. Let's assume you have passed the evaluation of your emotional commitment through communication and commonality. Now, how does your relationship fare with the thermometer of contractual commitment? Have you developed a habit of keeping promises, even little ones? Can you count on your partner to do what he or she says? Can your partner count on you? This is extremely important.

Many relationships have problems because the couple never thought of evaluating fidelity to both spoken and unspoken promises. If you have been dating for several months, you know whether or not you can count on your partner. You must consider each other's integrity. Remember, the rest of your life is a long time, and that's how long you plan to live with the person you marry. Integrity is no small matter. If you or your partner has a difficult time keeping promises, large or small, you should think twice about whether a marital promise will be kept! Jesus had a saying, "He who is faithful in a very little thing is also faithful in much; and he who is dishonest in a very little thing is also dishonest in much."

You can discover your partner's potential marital faithfulness by his or her faithfulness in "little things." This is what Jesus was getting at. *Little things are not so little when we understand them as part of a greater picture.* Little promises kept weave a network of high fidelity. Little promises broken start an unraveling process that is hard to stop. The question here is simple: can you and your partner be trusted to do what you say?

Trust

I was just recently asked, "What do you consider to be the single most important quality in a relationship or marriage?" A year ago I might have responded differently, but within the last year I have become convinced that the *single most important quality in a relationship is TRUST.* Trust gives us the freedom to be open and vulnerable; it gives us confidence to commit to someone; and it fills an empty hole in our soul.

It doesn't take long "out there in the real world" to realize that most everybody is looking out for number one. Oh, several will give us love, but we discover that it is given most often in moments of convenience. We soon feel somewhat isolated and alone. An emptiness in the pit of our gut drives us to cry out for just one person who really gives a rip, who cares about us, and whom we can trust to be there. Through the stages of a relationship you obtain the data of trustworthiness.

But the measure of trustworthiness must come from *trust experienced, and not merely trust expressed!* We must have witnessed that someone is worthy of our trust. The familiar phrase, "Trust me!" is wholly inadequate without the action to support it. Look back on your relationship. Has he kept his promises? Has she been there when you needed her? Does he really care about you? Or, is he more interested in himself? Has she demonstrated that she is worthy of trust?

As I discussed in the last chapter, one of the strongest attributes of my marriage is found in my wife's fidelity to me and to her promises. I know that no matter how tough things get she will always be with me. I have no fear of her ever walking out on me. Now, I am a realist. I am aware that life is a fickle journey, and I admit that just about anything is possible. For that very reason my wife's trustworthiness is even more wonderful. In a world where nothing is "for sure," it is a breath of life to find one person to count on. *A faithful and loving mate may be this world's closest thing to the faithful love of God*—a love we all seek.

The bottom line of bottom lines: After going through the process (stages) can you trust this person? And, can he or she trust you?

Dangers in the Stage

The Roping Stage is significant because the decisions that are made here will affect the rest of your life. The dangers, if we don't see them, can be very costly. There are three dangers that can lead to an unwise decision about potential marriage: unrealistic expectations, lover's blindness and constant conflict.

Unrealistic Expectations

Two common, unrealistic expectations have the potential of destroying a marriage: 1. Once we are married everything will work itself out; and 2. My partner and I will change after we are married.

One of the most dangerous things we can do is to expect

that our partner will change after we are married. I once counseled a couple who, in my opinion, were not at all ready for marriage. There was no communication, little trust and little respect for one another. I was growing very concerned. So I gave them special assignments to do at home. But each session they would return and report that they had not even attempted the assignments. Their response to me was, "We'll have plenty of time to do that stuff after we're married." Growing frustrated and more concerned, I tried to point out reality to them by asking, "Do you like your relationship the way it is right now? Would you be content to spend the rest of your life with each other, getting along exactly the way you do now?" Both of them immediately answered, "No, of course not, but it will get better." To this I said, "Wrong! You can never expect that your relationship will ever be any better than it is at this moment."

All we have to go on is what we have right now. Can't we hope for growth in our relationships? Sure, but only if we have been witnessing growth all along. *We can never expect that we will work any harder than we do right now.* We *might* work harder in the future, but it is unwise to expect that we will. Expectations such as that couple's are like New Year's resolutions; they seldom come to fruition. That is why we must have realistic expectations about a potential spouse. How do we develop realistic expectations? We develop them by evaluating the relationship with the three thermometers already discussed.

Lover's Blindness

The lover's blindness danger is directly related to unrealistic expectations. Because it is so dangerous, however, it warrants its own section. Lover's blindness is when one of the partners is so desperately in love with the other that he or she fails to see destructive habits, such as alcoholism, drug abuse, violent anger or a disrespect for life and people. The psychological and emotional reasons that cause someone to fall into this danger are varied and are beyond the scope of this book, but it is a common danger.

My pastoral heart comes out now as I plead with you to be wise. Do not ignore the obvious. If someone has a substance abuse or people abuse problem, do not marry him or her until the problem has been worked out. Living with an abuser, whether the abuse is toward self or others, can be a hell on earth. Never, never expect someone to change just because you are getting married. Rather, ask yourself honestly, "What will my life be like when this person is at his worst?" because history shows the situation will be worse after you are married.

Constant Conflict

Every relationship has conflict, or it is not even a relationship. An entire chapter will be devoted to managing normal, healthy conflict. But conflict is unhealthy when a couple spends more than half the time fighting and arguing.

If a relationship is marked by constant conflict, it's wise to ask, "Are we really good for each other? Is there something missing in our commonality or rapport?" Sometimes we stay in relationships for the wrong reasons—habit, convenience, fear of hurting or being hurt, fear of loneliness. A couple once told me, "We're great at resolving our conflicts; we just have to do it all the time." They seemed to live in constant conflict.

I have observed an interesting dilemma in some relationships. On the one hand, the couple has developed great openness, vulnerability and trust. They have discovered sacred safety with each other. But on the other hand, they have major gaps in commonality; they have different interests and values. What should they do? Should they get married? Only the couple can provide the answer. My advice is reasonably simple. First, avoid the question, "How can I live without you?" Believe it or not, you can live (and live well) without any one particular person. The question to ask is, "Can I spend the rest of my life with you, getting along the way we do?"

Breaking Up?

What do you do when your relationship has grown all the way to the Roping Stage and you decide that marriage is not the best option? Or, what about relationships that go through the Scoping Stage and find that it is not good to go any further? Remember, very, very few relationships ever go past the Scoping Stage, nor should they. How do you decide to call it quits? Is there an easy way to do it? The answer, unfortunately, is no; there is no easy way to break up with someone. It is one of the most difficult things we ever have to do. But while there is no easy way, there is a good way, using tempered honesty and kindness.

Before you break up, take the time to evaluate why the relationship is not working. The information on the stages is helpful in making that evaluation. If you are sure it is time to end the relationship, you owe it to your friend to discuss it. It is tragic to end a relationship with a curt phone call, or even worse, just to disappear. In relationships that have gone at least through the Scoping Stage, you owe communication to your friend. It will be tough, but it must be done, and with tempered honesty. Don't be vicious in telling someone why you no longer want to spend time with him or her. Show kindness and respect. The Golden Rule is the goal; treat others the way you would like them to treat you.

A Final Word

Before getting married there are four questions you should be able to answer affirmatively. If you can't say yes to all these questions, you need to reevaluate your decision to marry.

1. Do you expect real things from each other and your relationship?

2. Do you have commitment and trust?

3. Do you communicate well?

4. Is your relationship marked by harmony?

If you have successfully gone through the stages and you can answer yes to all four questions, then marriage is a viable option for you. Making the decision to call it love or call it quits is tough, but it can be done wisely. The stages can be helpful. Use them well.

9

Stage Fright

"I don't understand what went wrong," Marsha sighed as she sat across from me in my counseling office. "Doug and I were getting so close. We spent hours talking. We were always together on weekends, walking on the beach or strolling around Balboa Island, you know, being so much in love. But now, well, we can't even talk to each other without fighting. I'm sure we're going to break up. Why, we even talked about getting married!"

I asked Marsha how long she and Doug had dated. "Four weeks," she told me. Four weeks! Four weeks! "Gimme a break," I thought to myself. Four weeks is hardly long enough to decide if you want to go on vacation with someone, much less marry him! At least you can fly home from a vacation.

Doug was suffering from Stage Fright. The stages of a relationship define the normal, natural process by which we move into meaningful relationships. But, sometimes the process gets scary. If we move too quickly through the stages, one person or the other may get frightened away. On the other hand we can become afraid of progressing at all and become stagnant. Stage Fright can be a problem at either of end of the spectrum.

Stage Fright is most often found in two common errors: Stage Jumping and Stage Stuck. Stage Jumping is skipping one of the stages and moving much too quickly in the relationship. This was Marsh and Doug's error. Stage Stuck is just the opposite; it's failing to move on to the next stage and so not progressing in the relationship. Both errors are common. In fact, I would guess that most people who read this book will have experienced both of the errors personally, and probably more than once.

Stage Jumping

Stage Jumping is a natural tendency when we meet a wonderful, exciting and affirming person. When we relate to someone so well, we ask, "Why wait? This is great; let's go for it." And so we charge into the relationship with all the gusto of Don Quixote and unfortunately get many of the same rewards—broken dreams and broken hearts. Our hunger for the ultimate relationship causes us to pass over some fundamental aspects of relating. We move from Hoping to Coping, or Scoping to Roping, or even Hoping to Roping. The end result is often tragic. We lose our relationship because we simply moved too fast.

Feeling Close

Stage Jumping often begins with the dangers explained in Chapter Six, "Too Much Too Soon" and "Too Deep Too Long." These dangers are more common to those personality types who have the ability to get very deep very quickly. They may spend entire evenings and until the wee hours of the morning just talking, about everything. They reveal very intimate secrets about themselves, and because they are often caring and compassionate people, they receive great warmth and affirmation from their new friend. All of this mutual self-disclosure and affirmation leads them to believe they have finally met the person of their dreams.

Within a matter of weeks (sometimes days) they become convinced that marriage is a great option in this relationship. Now, it's all right to think about marrying someone; the problem comes when they start acting like engaged people after only a few weeks of dating. Expectations are placed on the relationship that it cannot bear; it has not had enough time under its belt.

Sex

Another reason people fall into the trap of jumping stages is sex. Few things in life are more immediately bonding than sex. Think about it. Would you take your clothes off in public? Or, would you walk up to your best friend, remove your clothing, and ask, "Well, what d'ya think?" Of course you wouldn't. And yet, that is exactly what we do when we engage in sex. We show another person our nakedness, our flaws, our imperfect bodies and, in a sense, we ask, "What d'ya think?" When the other person responds with tenderness and acceptance, it is an incredibly bonding experience.

And so the obvious danger. Our relationship is built around our bodies. We feel close because we are close, but incompletely so. Sex begins to be misused. Problems are solved by sex; entertainment is found in sex. Intimacy and sexual activity appear to be synonymous—one of the most dangerous lies propagated on modern mankind. Sex is only one of the many aspects of intimacy, but we can't see that when we are in the middle of it. Because there is such a feeling of closeness, the couple naturally begins to think of marriage, or at least of serious commitment much too soon, within a few short weeks, or even days.

The danger really heightens when a couple is involved in both: real deep real fast, emotionally and sexually. Some may ask, "What's wrong with that? If a couple talks deeply and shares sensitive, caring and monogamous sex, aren't they on a path of great growth in their relationship?" No, actually they are probably heading for a rocky path. Let me explain why.

Skipping Scoping

If a couple has been together a very short time, it is counterproductive to place too much commitment on the relationship. Common errors are made:

1. *Immediate Exclusivity.* I have nothing against monogamous dating. In fact, my preference is that people date only one person at a time. But the error is to expect exclusive commitment from one another too soon. A relationship in its early stages is not ready for too many boundaries. Often one or both of the partners begin to feel closed in or boxed up. It is better to allow exclusivity to evolve more naturally.

2. *Immediate Coupling.* Closely related to immediate exclusivity is immediate coupling. The new couple and their friends begin to act as if they were almost married when they are still a long way from marriage.

3. *Expected Presence.* Viewing themselves as a couple, each begins to expect the presence of the other at certain gatherings (weddings, office parties) and on certain days (Friday, Saturday and Sunday). Phone calls, cards and flowers are often expected. Usually the pace is more than either can bear.

When we place great expectations on a relationship too early, we inevitably fail to meet the expectations, and then trust is broken. In the example of Marsha, Doug could no longer live up to the expectations each of them had placed on the relationship. It was too heavy a demand.

An interesting thing occurs in Stage Jumping. The expectations placed on a young relationship are often more stringent than those placed on great marriages. Expectations placed on young relationships are usually based on egocentric need—what I expect the relationship to look like. Oh, we discuss expectations with our partner, but *people in new relationships are uncommonly agreeable.* Expectations found in more mature relationships are based more on what the couple, in reality, is capable of fulfilling. *Expectations are grown into, not devised.*

Fallen Fruit Tree

A relationship that jumps stages can look like a fruit tree loaded with tasty, delicious fruit. All we see are ripe, juicy and inviting delights that we must have, and now: affirmation, sexuality and acceptance. The problem is that the tree has not had time to develop a deep and solid root system: commitment and unwavering acceptance, in spite of faults. Therefore, while it looks marvelous, it is actually frail and weak. Any wind of trial and "it's a gonner." We all long to be truly known, and loved anyway. It just can't happen without time.

How Much Time?

How much time is enough time before getting married? How long does it take to go through the stages? I hesitate to include this section because some will see it as a rule. I am not a rule maker; that job belongs to someone else. What I am about to say is my opinion. I think it's a good opinion, but that's for you to judge. I believe the minimum time it takes to go through the stages is six months, and I do mean minimum; I think the process works best over the period of about one year. Still, it can be done in six months depending on the maturity of the individuals involved.

Why do I say six months to one year? Each of us is very capable of being someone else for a short period of time (one, two, three, four months). We are capable of being a people pleaser for a short period of time. If our partner wants a sensitive lover, we can do that for a while even if we don't like it. But we can't be someone else forever. Eventually the real person must surface. And it is the real person we must live with in a marriage.

Also, it is good to experience seasons of life with a person to see what he or she is like. The longer we are with someone the more opportunities we have to see what he or she is like in different situations. We learn a lot about character. If there is a very short courtship, we might be surprised at whom we married. Six months to one year seems to give ample time for evaluation.

Stage Stuck

Do you have friends who have been in a relationship that just seemed to go on and on without ever going anywhere? Have you ever been in such a relationship, one that seemed to be stuck for months, or for two, three, four, five years or longer? These relationships have become Stage Stuck. They are in a rut; growth has not occurred for a long time, and they are stagnant. These relationships are "just there."

Just There

The stage that most relationships get stuck in is Scoping, and sometimes early Coping. The couple will grow well through the Hoping Stage and then grow more vulnerable and accepting in the Scoping Stage, but then get stuck before moving on to the Coping Stage. The fear of commitment is often the culprit and Chapter Eleven will deal with that fear.

As in other areas of our lives, we, like a stream, are prone to take the path of least resistance in our relationships. It's the easy way that avoids and evades. Working through the Coping Stage is hard work. Sometimes we have to do things we don't necessarily want to do. We might have to give up some of our ego, of getting things our way. So, it's easier just to stay the way we are. The relationship moves into a dangerous comfort zone.

Relationships that fail to move on to the Coping Stage become relationships of habit and convenience. It's like a guarantee that someone will be there. The problem is that they are "just there," just a body, barely warm.

Getting Stuck Deeper

A fact of life is that there are no such things as plateaus; we never get "to arrive." We are always en route, one way or the other. If we are stuck in a relationship, we are really on a downhill slide; it may be a slow slide, but it's a slide nevertheless. So, what happens in this kind of relationship? A relationship that is stuck, without progressive moves, will only get stuck deeper.

In the last chapter I pointed out that the single most important quality in a relationship is trust. If there is no growth in trust and commitment, an emptiness develops in the relationship. After months and years one, or both, of the partners begin to wonder how long the other is going to be around. Trust is deeply eroded.

What follows is tragic. The couple begins to develop terrible relational habits because of the low commitment and waning trust. A habit develops of always (consciously or unconsciously) questioning the reliability of the other. Horrible fights usually result. But because the known is more comfortable than the unknown, the relationship continues; it just never grows.

How Long Is Too Long?

I am really sticking my neck out on this one. How long is too long is a very personal question. The answer depends on the depth and maturity of the individuals and of the relationship. However, I do have a rule of thumb that I offer people: two years should be the limit. After two years of dating we probably have all the data we could ever hope to gather about the other person. We have witnessed great evolution in our relationship.

I have seen too many unhappy people who have become Stage Stuck. It seems the longer they stay together the more difficult the decision for marriage is. Many good relationships

A fact of life is that there are no such things as plateaus; we never get "to arrive." We are always en route, one way or the other.

have been ruined by waiting too long. After years and years of dating they not only have established bad relational habits, they also have learned everything there is to know about their partner.

Is it possible to learn too much about a partner? Yes, what we learn too much about is details, not disposition; circumstances, not character. In many years of unmarried relationship each person sees the other at his or her worst, more as a spectator than as a participant. In many years of marriage one partner sees the other at his or her worst, but as a participant, working through the issues because survival dictates that they do so. So while trials can bond a marriage, they can break a relationship that refuses to make the commitment for the long haul.

I feel strongly that two years is long enough to call it love or call it quits. An exception to the two year limit is college students. I think that something different is going on in a relationship during the student years. But after college the rule of thumb applies.

Living Together

Why get married when you can live together? That is the question of the day! In my ministry I counsel many people who come from a nonchurch background. And why not? I, too, come from a nonchurch background; I didn't darken the doors of a church until I was thirty years old. But I have been amazed at the number of people living together before marriage. I recently had a string of premarital counseling sessions where eight out of ten couples were already living together by the time they had come to see me. I thought that living together went out with the twist. Boy, was I wrong. And for those of you who are actively involved in your local church, don't get too snooty. I find that the people living together before marriage is not limited to the nonchurched.

Couples who are living together and not married are generally in stuck relationships. They came together with wonderful, but ideal, motives: we will love each other until we don't or let's find out if we really love each other or let's evaluate our compatibility by living together. The problem is obvious. They are merely playing house, playing at marriage. We need more security in our relationships. We need to know that our mate is going to be there "come Robert Redford or Raquel Welch." Loving only because we feel like it, by definition, assumes a precarious level of commitment, and trust. We simply cannot trust someone who may walk out the door just because they felt like it was time to walk out the door.

I believe the creation intent for the male-female bond was for a woman and a man to be committed for life. The writer of Genesis in speaking of the male-female bond said, "For this reason a man will leave his father and mother and be united to his wife, and they will become one flesh." In paraphrase, "A man should leave the dominion of his father and mother and set up camp with his wife. The two of them should be so uniquely united that they will become spiritually and emotionally as one person." This is the way a male-female relationship works—the only way it works! It takes a mutual commitment to love and longevity. Becoming "one flesh" is not temporary.

Oddly enough, living together actually sabotages the goals of most relationships. When a couple lives together as an experiment, they often find that the experiment was doomed to fail from its inception because of two missing ingredients. I'm sure that by now you can guess what those missing ingredients might be: commitment and trust. Trust is what we need and search for in every relationship. But how can we trust without commitment? How can we trust someone to do something that they never agreed to do? We can't, and our relationship suffers because of it.

I counsel a lot of couples who are living together and who

have discovered a great emptiness in their relationship. They have a tough time moving on to meaningful commitment because they have developed bad relational habits. But it is a switch they must make if they have any hope at all for their relationship. None of them denies their great desire for trust, while feeling an emptiness in their lives for the lack of it.

If you are living together, my caution is to do one of two things. Get married and make the lifelong commitment that can give you life. Or, if you are not ready to get married, then get out. Move out and save your relationship because the longer you stay in your current situation the less chance you have of your relationship surviving. God's program really does work. He is not a capricious God who makes unreasonable rules. He is the Creator of all things, and he has given us the handbook for survival. He has also spoken to us about how best to honor him. We are most like him when we keep our promises, not when we avoid promises and sidetrack creation intent. Staying out of an unmarried living situation just makes sense. It's your best choice—relationally and spiritually.

10

Permanence: Privilege or Prohibition?

In 1980 there were 18,178 marriages in Orange County, California. While these 18,000 couples were celebrating the joy of their new union, another 12,676 couples were throwing in the towel saying, "I quit. I've had it. Goodbye." For every nine marriages in Orange County there are six divorces. Records show that at least 45 percent of all marriages in the U.S. will end in divorce and, what's even worse, 55 percent of all second marriages will not make it.

The word out of Las Vegas (the world's largest marriage factory) is, "When you get married, make sure you do it early in the morning. That way if it doesn't work out, you haven't ruined a whole day." Levity in the midst of disaster.

It's scary to think you have barely a 50 percent chance of survival. It's scary to think you might commit to something you later will hate. Marriage is a scary deal. In fact, anything permanent is scary. In our mobile society we want to grow, experience new places and new people. We want adventure. But, as we discussed in the previous section, we cannot grow without permanence. Commitment is the foundation for personal growth.

Any way you look at it, a book on relationships must deal with the issue of permanence. Permanence is something we all long for in the depths of our soul. We want something we can count on. We need *someone* we can count on. Jim Loder, a professor at Princeton University, says we spend our entire lives looking for "a face that won't go away." When we are tiny infants, the only thing we see in life is Mother's face that comes (and gives us love) and then goes away again—coming and going, coming and going. Our lives are a search for that face that won't go away. The face we are looking for is the face of God. We find the face of God in several ways, primarily in the face of Jesus, but secondarily in the faces of committed people. Our spouses are the most tangible sign of the face that won't go away. No wonder divorce is so devastating.

Permanence is a privilege, not a prohibition. It is the route to a meaningful relationship. Without permanence, love is reduced to narcissism—getting the good stuff and leaving when it takes some work.

11

The Fears of Commitment

I was in my office one afternoon daydreaming, as usual, when I received a phone call. The voice on the other end seemed disturbed, almost frantic. "Are you the expert on commitment phobia?"

"Am I the what?" I questioned. I had recently completed a series of lectures on "Finding Friends and Making Mates." In one of the lectures I had discussed some fears of commitment. I guess that made me an expert.

My desperate caller went on, "I need your help. I've been dating a girl for two and a half years, and I just can't make up my mind whether I want to marry her. I think I'm a commitment phobic. Can you help me?"

Up to that time I had never even heard the term "commitment phobic," but I had met scores of people with the symptoms. Many people have an almost phobic reaction to the idea of commitment. "Commitment" seems to be the longest four-letter word in the dictionary. Some people pass out at the sound of it.

Commitment phobia (and I use the term tongue-in-cheek, not clinically) begins rather innocently. For some, it initially sprouts right after high school when they feel it is not the right time to marry because they must either pursue a career or a college education. Those who go on to college finally graduate and say, "I can't get married now. I have so much invested in my education that now I have to get my career in line." (And rarely does the career seem to get in line.) Here the problem begins to show its ugly little head. Our career person is now in his or her late twenties or early thirties and doesn't know how to develop a lasting relationship. Oh, he knows how to date and have fun. He knows how to get close to a meaningful relationship, but he doesn't know how to make one last. Or, she has spent so much time avoiding commitments that now she isn't sure where to start. Yet somewhere deep within is this gnawing urge to get involved.

With others, commitment phobia begins with the deep pain experienced in broken commitments. Some have been hurt by unsuccessful relationships, others by divorce. And the hurt doesn't go totally away. It lingers and builds until it eventually becomes a wall.

What are we afraid of in relationships? Why are so many people failing to make the final leap, the leap to commitment? I believe there are two major barriers that prevent people from making the commitment necessary for lasting relationships. The barriers are fears of commitment and follies about commitment.

Half of any battle is knowing our enemy. This chapter will help us recognize our first enemy: the fears of commitment. It will even point out some ideas for remedy. In the next chapter we will take a look at our second enemy: the follies, or misperceptions, about commitment. Any way we look at it, we must realize this: it is impossible to have a meaningful relationship without commitment.

Admittedly, if I were to list all of the various fears of commitment, the list would be endless. But I like to think in big pictures. I like synthesis. So, I have synthesized the fears of commitment into three major groupings: the fear of failure, the fear of being hindered and the fear of being hurt.

The Fear of Failure

When statistics indicate there is a 50 percent chance of failure in marriage, many people become overcautious. No one wants to go through divorce. We all have friends who have been divorced, and we have watched their great pain and emotional upheaval. Many of us have personally experienced divorce and know the horror of it. Fear of failure in a marriage is one of the most common fears unmarried people face.

The Longer You Wait the Harder It Is

Who do you think has a greater fear of failure in a marriage—a person over thirty who has never been married or a person over thirty who has been divorced? Generally, the immediate response is the person who has been divorced because he or she has felt so much pain. But my counseling experience has led me to believe that is not the case. I have found that the longer people wait to get married the greater their fear of failure becomes.

Nobody wants to end up a statistic, unless it's a good one, like the 50 percent of marriages that survive. People who have waited a long time to be married seem to have unusually heightened fears of marital failure. They fall prey to the "what if" syndrome. What if he turns out to be a jerk? What if I fall out of love with her? What if five years down the road we end up hating each other? What if somebody better comes along after we're married?

The problem with "what if" questions is that they are, to a degree, unanswerable. We don't have a crystal ball; nobody does. We have no guarantees about the future. Ironically, the fact that we have no guarantees can actually insure the success of a marriage because without guarantees we are left with only one option—love, hard-working, committed love. People who have failed to make commitments earlier in life become increasingly fearful of commitments as time goes on.

People who have made commitments and failed understand the reality of it. They often know where they made mistakes in the past and are prepared to deal with them better the next time.

All of us are burdened with the fear of failure. The only way I know to compensate for the fear is to risk wisely. The stages of a relationship provide a base from which we can do that.

The Fear of Being Hindered

This particular fear belongs largely to males, although some women suffer from it also. The fear of being hindered is the fear that if I make a commitment now, I am forever stuck. What if someone better comes along? What if I change my mind later? It's the idea that "the grass is greener on the other side of the hill," but the reality of the matter is that the "grass is sometimes brown on both sides."

The Myth of Limitation

Two major myths surround this fear. One is that commitment is too limiting, that it prevents us from experiencing all that life has to offer. No wonder we buy into this myth. We have been inculcated with it for the last twenty to thirty years. Manufacturers and advertisers capitalize on making us believe that newer is nicer and bigger is better. Just think of the phrases that are used to market products: "new and improved," "newest formula," "latest research." We have been programmed to believe that something better will always come along, and we naturally transfer the concept to our relationships.

The problem with this myth is that if we are always looking for something better, we will sure enough run into something that at first glance appears to be better. A mystique surrounds a new person or a new relationship. But I challenge you to think back on all the people you were really excited about when you first met them, people you at first thought would be great to date. And then after you got to know them, you discovered what jerks they really were. We are easily mesmerized by our own imaginations, and we too often make people out to be more than they are.

The Myth of Preventive Permanence

A second myth that surrounds the fear of being hindered is similar to the first. This myth says permanence prevents growth. In her wonderful little children's story *A Wind In The Door*, Madeleine L'Engle describes fascinating little creatures called "farandolae" who love to flit around from person to person, country to country, planet to planet and galaxy to galaxy. The worst imaginable thing in the eyes of young farandolae is to be stuck in one place. As the tension mounts by the end of the story, we discover that all human life depends upon the young farandolae doing exactly what they fear most, becoming permanent, being in one spot. Ironically, it is then, and only then, that the young creatures become truly free because it is then that they "Deepen" and mature. L'Engle says, "Once a farandolae has Deepened he will no longer have to run about."

We are like the young farandolae. Once we have "deepened," we will no longer have to run about. But we often hate the idea of permanence. We feel as if we are stuck and can never again grow, when the irony of the matter is that the only way we truly can grow is through permanence and commitment. Destroying these two myths is an important part of learning maturity.

Men and Many Dates

I said before that the fear of being hindered is most common among males. It helps to understand just why this is so. Men receive a large part of their identity and self-esteem from their achievements and accomplishments, i.e. career, titles, athletics, awards and women they date. Some men like to date more than one woman at a time because, by doing so, they believe they are better people and more valuable men.

The idea of commitment can hit a sensitive nerve. A man may fear that making a commitment to one person will limit the number of his "accomplishments" and "achievements" (dates) and somehow he will become less of a man. He will no longer be free to date whomever he pleases. He will no longer be able to accomplish the world's greatest feat by getting the world's most desired woman (someone who, by the way, doesn't exist). So there can be an underlying fear that he might be hindered from being the best man he could possibly be.

Let me make a note here for those who have questions or arguments with my statements about men. First, more often than not, the drive to date many women to build self-esteem is a predominately unconscious drive. A person isn't usually aware of the dynamic unless he stops and analyzes the situation. Second, not all men feel they must date many women in order to satisfy personal identity needs. Still, it is common among men. Third, women are not immune to the problem. Some women are motivated by very similar drives.

The fear of being hindered is a very American phenomenon. We have so much available at our fingertips. We want to taste everything we see. We cheer, "Life is to enjoy!" While life is to enjoy, we cut ourselves off from the joy by refusing to recognize the deep and lasting joy which results from relational commitment.

The Fear of Being Hurt

When I was twenty-three years old, after a year and a half of marriage, I went through a separation and divorce. I made some bad mistakes in my first marriage. I caused a lot of pain and I received a lot of pain. After the divorce I swore I would never again go through that kind of pain. I did not want to hurt anyone, nor did I want to be hurt. As a result, I spent the next decade either running from relationships or sabotaging them. I used to date several women at a time so that I didn't have to get involved. I had a little guideline for myself. If I dated anyone more than two times in the same month, I had to be careful because she might think I liked her. And if she thought I liked her, she had the ammo to hurt me. I wasn't going to give anyone that edge. So I was a very lonely man.

Our fear of being hurt may be the greatest enemy of successful relationships. One of the hardest pains on earth is the pain of a lover's rejection. When my friend Terry Hershey does his divorce recovery seminars, he titles them, "Beginning Again." He invites all people who have suffered from a relational loss, whether through divorce or breakup. He is one of the few people who understands that a lover's rejection is part and parcel to divorce. The pain of a broken relationship is in many ways just as traumatic.

With that pain we build a little protective wall around our heart, and every now and then we peek out to see if it's safe. If we get hurt a second time, we make our wall a little higher and a little wider. With every hurt the wall grows to be more like a fortress until we finally end up doing what I did for ten years—running and wrecking. And we become very lonely people.

We don't have to be immobilized by our fears. Believe it or not, we do have a choice in this matter. We can control these fears. The first step is to name them, recognize them for what they are. Let's look at three of them: the pain of unreciprocated love, the pain of being used and the pain of desertion.

Our fear of being hurt may be the greatest enemy of successful relationships.

The Pain of Unreciprocated Love

In human relationships, love given is incomplete love. Love cannot fully develop until it is received and responded to. We want to be met halfway in a relationship, and we feel naked and exposed if our partner does not reciprocate when we give our affections. We fear giving someone our unswerving love and having him or her still hang around without returning the same kind of love. This turns into a very one-sided relationship with us on the wrong side.

We fear telling someone we love him or her only to have this person respond with a very different message like, "I wish you hadn't said that." I know a man who once was sitting in the car with a woman, trying to tell her how much he cared for her while she was saying, "Don't do this. I don't want to hear this." We want to be liked to at least the same degree that we like the other person. If that doesn't occur, we feel overexposed and undervalued.

The fear of having our love unreciprocated prevents us from taking a chance with someone we have become very fond of.

The Pain of Being Used

Have you ever been taken advantage of by someone you really cared about? Have you given someone your heart only to have him or her use your love against you? It can be devastating. Most people are not malicious. Most people do not intentionally take advantage of others with whom they are in relationship. Nevertheless, we are afraid that someone will take advantage of us if we give them information that makes us vulnerable. And, if we have ever been burned in this area, we are even more cautious. We can reduce the risk and fear of being used by taking wise steps in self-revelation.

The Pain of Desertion

The fear of desertion is one of the most paralyzing fears in a relationship, especially if we have been deserted in the past. We ask ourselves, "What if I do give my love to this person? What guarantee do I have that he won't walk?" The underlying fear is the fear of rejection.

I counsel a lot of single people who are involved in various levels of relationships. The greatest hurt I see is the hurt that comes from breaking up, from rejection or desertion. We all want guarantees before we go into our relationships, guarantees that our partner won't leave us. The unfortunate truth, however, is that life offers no such guarantees. But we can't allow that to prevent us from taking some relational risks.

Cautious, Not Closed

Everyone who reads this book has been hurt in a relationship. There is no way to avoid it. We are each too brittle on the one hand and too insensitive to others on the other hand not to hurt each other. And let me tell you an absolute fact of life. Unless you die within the next twenty-four hours, you will be hurt again! Great news? Hardly. Still, it is a fact of life. But we don't have to go through life as a doormat for other people's relational abuse. What, then, are our options?

While there are no guarantees, there are precautions we can take. We can enter into our relationships with wisdom. In order to have a meaningful relationship, we must take risks. But we don't have to risk the whole farm; we can offer a chicken or a duck, not the entire lower forty. The wisdom to properly handle a relationship is found in the stages (the process) we discussed in the previous section of this book.

Our fears don't necessarily have to be roadblocks to our relationships. Instead, we can use our fears wisely. If a child gets burned by a stove, does that mean the child will never cook with fire? Of course not. But that child will never again stick his hand in the flame. That's what we want to learn from the past—to keep our hands out of the flame. But we have to cook. Learn from your fears. Be cautious without being closed.

12

The Follies About Commitment

I recently saw a wonderfully entertaining movie, *Three Men and a Baby*. While this movie was cute and endearing, it also propagated a popular American cultural folly—the single, uncommitted, playboy/playgirl life-style is great. There is no greater lie in the world today. I was a single, adult male for seventeen years (thirteen of which were as far away from "religion" as one could get). In my experience I never once knew a "playboy/playgirl" who enjoyed that life-style for any extended period of time. Oh, I imagine there are some out there somewhere, but I never found them, and I got around!

We are not created to be alone and uncommitted. We are created to be in an intimate relationship, physically, emotionally and spiritually. I think *Three Men and a Baby* pointed out our innate need for relationship and procreation. It failed, however, to point out our innate desire to be in a parental/marital relationship, father-mother, husband-wife, lover-lover.

I am not suggesting that a single adult cannot live a meaningful and fulfilled life. Many do. I am saying a single adult cannot *pretend* at relationship, that is, live the uncommitted, single playboy/playgirl life and expect to find it meaningful. There are some follies about commitment which lead us away from the very committed relationship we desire. These follies relate to how we view ourselves, our needs and our relationships with other people. They are the folly of false reality, the folly of eternality and the folly of individuality.

The Folly of False Reality

The Perfect Person

A very dear friend of mine once told me a whimsical story about himself. "I dated a lot of interesting women in my time," he said, "but I never got close enough for marriage. Then one day I woke up and looked in the mirror, and I suddenly realized I wasn't Tom Selleck. So I finally asked myself, 'Why was I looking for Bo Derek?' "

I think it's funny that we all want to find a "ten" when most of us are only a "six," at best. We want the perfect person and the perfect relationship. Now, I know that some of you are disagreeing with me by saying, "Not me. I'm a realist. I know there is no such thing as a perfect person. I would never expect my partner to be perfect." Let me challenge you on that. While it may be true that you don't want *the* perfect person, you do want *your* perfect person. In an earlier chapter I talked about our lists and how each of us has a list of traits we want and don't want in a partner. That list defines *your* perfect person.

It's quite possible that even in *your* perfect person your sights are too high. Too many women and men are looking for Bo Derek and Tom Selleck and are passing up excellent relational prospects like the boy or girl next door, or the person you are currently dating. I have seen too many great relationships die because one of the partners was looking for their "ten." Unfortunately most often the struggle is solely with physical attractiveness. I hear comments like, "I just don't feel the fireworks," or "I'm not turned on by him," or even, "I struggle because she's not pretty enough."

"Not pretty enough!" I respond. "Who do you think you are?" The struggle of physical attractiveness betrays a very sad phenomenon—the terribly weak ego of the "eye of the beholder."

I had a professor once who pointed out a disturbing attribute of couples in our culture: we use our partner as a tool to make us look good. A man wants a "ten" in order to make *him* look good in public; a woman wants a witty man in order to make *her* look good at a party; we all want influential partners who will make *us* look good in the eyes of others. But what about our lives behind closed doors, where the opinions of others don't count? That is where we live most of our lives—in relationship, and looks matter little. As I said before, the longer a couple is together the less looks become an issue.

The Perfect Relationship

Another folly of false reality is the idea of a perfect relationship, one that doesn't have conflict or one that doesn't have times of great frustration. Remember this, relationship is hard work. There is no such thing as a relationship that doesn't have conflict or where the couple doesn't sometimes wonder if it is a mistake to be together. Struggles are perfectly normal.

You Can't Love a Perfect Person

The folly of false reality is a deterrent to commitment and the joy of intimate relationship. I once counseled a young couple who had been together for several years. The young woman wanted to call it love or call it quits, but the young man was suffering from commitment phobia. After a few sessions I asked him what he had learned thus far from our time together. He said that he understood for the first time that nobody was perfect and that he had no right to expect perfection from his girlfriend.

A light went off in my head, and something profound occurred to me. Even if he were to find the perfect person, he would not be able to love her. He could adore her, worship her and be proud of her, but he could not love her. You see, perfection contradicts the very basis of love; it defies the definition of love. Love is learning to accept, live with and even

Love is being known well and loved anyway.

appreciate the peculiarities of another person. Love is forgiving and being forgiven. Love is being known well and loved anyway. If we were to find a perfect person, we would lose the wonder of love.

The Folly of Eternality

The folly of eternality comes from the idea that "I have all the time in the world to get married." My friend that I mentioned earlier also told me that at forty-one years old he realized he wasn't going to live forever, that he too could die. Life is much shorter than we think it is. The older we get the more we understand how true that is. We have to be very careful about thinking we have more time than we know what to do with. Because before we know it, we will be old . . . and alone.

Another factor deters commitment from people who think they have all the time in the world. It is the idea that "I've waited this long to get married. So, unless I find the perfect person for me, I can wait some more." Or, I have even heard, "Why should I marry him when I turned down better five years ago?" The longer we wait the pickier we get, until finally we get to a point that nobody will ever pass our stringent code.

The readers who should be especially careful here are those currently in their twenties. It is in the twenties that we establish the basis for the folly. When I was in my twenties, there was little urgency in life, especially when it came to relationships. I felt that time was on my side, and in many ways it was. But I encourage you not to pass up a wonderful person just because you feel "you aren't ready yet." If you have developed a successful relationship, I caution you not to let it slip away. Great relationships are difficult to find. It may be a long time before you find another. Be aware of the folly of eternality before it sneaks up on you.

The Folly of Individuality

The final folly that keeps us from making intimate commitments is what I have called "the cult of the autonomous individual." This, too, is a very American folly. It begins with the belief that I can do anything in the world I want to do on my own; I don't need other people; I am an individual. And it results in the notion that life revolves around me. That really is a treacherous deception. There is nothing in the world we need more than other people.

I Don't Need Anyone

I get very nervous whenever I hear someone make the remark, "I don't need anyone." This book is dedicated to the notion that we are all desperately needy people, desperately in need of other people. We need to be heard, accepted and cared for. We need to be in intimate relationship. Through relationship we grow and develop and learn about life. Don't let yourself buy into the lie that says you can do anything in the world you want to do and you don't need anyone to help get you there. It quite simply is not true.

I have met only a few people who had no desire to marry. This very fact testifies to the folly of individuality. If we want to be married, then we do indeed need other people. We must admit our need because it gets us going in the right direction in relationships; it moves us toward intimacy.

Antidote to the Follies

The follies of false reality, eternality and individuality all deny truth. You are not perfect (but neither is anyone else), you will get old, and you do need other people. To believe the follies is to believe a deception, to follow the road to loneliness. The best antidote to the follies is to see life for what it really is, an opportunity to love and be loved.

In order to love, you will have to take a few risks. Maybe your partner isn't perfect, maybe you will fail, but you won't ever know unless you try. But try wisely. Let me offer two simple suggestions. First, be realistic. There is no perfect person, you will get old and you do need other people. Admit that life is what it really is. Second, risk wisely. Use the stages of a relationship as your guide to discover your compatibility with a potential spouse.

The real issue that lies at the bottom of our fears and follies is our *desire for control*. We want things to be done our way and we want guarantees; we don't like the unknown. And yet, it is impossible not to have an enormous number of uncontrollable variables in our lives. When we look at life honestly, we realize just how little control we really do have. I think of Richard Nixon and the 1972 presidential election. Mr. Nixon won that election by the largest landslide ever in a presidential election. Who would have guessed that only two years later he would be forced to leave office! Just when it seemed he was in a moment of great control, his life fell out from under him.

There is a paradox. On the one hand, we have influence in our own lives. We can appropriate wisdom, and our relationships likely will be good. On the other hand, no one has absolute control; life is fickle. The fear of the unknown is something we must continue to face on this side of eternity. As a minister, I enjoy the "unknown" in my life. It adds excitement, but more importantly, the unknown in my life is what I call "God-room."

It doesn't take long for us to realize that we, ultimately, have limited control in life. That creates within us a sense of dependency. When I come face to face with the unknown in my life, I take comfort in the fact that there is Someone who does have control and as the psalmist says, "How precious are your thoughts about me, O God! How vast is the sum of them. If I were to count them, they would outnumber the sand" (Psalm 139:17).

13

Commitment vs. Convenience

Commitment versus convenience. It's the battle of quality versus quantity. The battle of long term versus short term. No one can escape this constant struggle in life. In analyzing this great battle, convenience needs no description or instruction about how it works. Convenience is as natural as can be. It is the path of least pain and most comfort. Therefore, no one needs training to go for convenience. On the other hand, commitment needs description and instruction because it isn't natural to us. Yet commitment is the only antidote for convenience.

If we are going to have permanence in a marriage relationship, or in any relationship for that matter, we have to be willing to make some commitments that fly in the face of convenience. We have already looked at two kinds of commitments—emotional commitments and contractual commitments—that we have to make to our partner if we are to progress this far in the stages of a relationship. But for there to be permanence in a relationship, we must *share* a commitment to priority living.

Priority living is learning to live life on purpose by the use of the most basic priorities. Priority living recognizes that some things are more important than others. If we can live our lives according to its priorities, we will grow personally, and in relationship to significant people in our lives, and in our professions.

It's been my experience that most people come to God by the process of elimination— nothing else works!

It's critical from the outset that we understand that no one can function consistently within his or her priorities. Just about the time we think we've got it going, someone will call or knock at the door. We will never "arrive" when it comes to priorities, but by the use of priorities, we will at least be in the process of arriving.

As we move through the relational stages, we should take care not to sell out short by coupling with someone who rejects this life strategy. Most relationships that end in disaster could have been avoided by a commitment to priority living. Making a commitment to priority living becomes a meaningful strategy for our lives and a measuring stick for evaluating others.

The First Priority: God

When I am counseling couples who have a strong commitment to developing intimacy, the first thing I encourage them to do is to establish a relationship with God together. Go on a spiritual search together. Read the Bible and discuss it. (Try Proverbs first!) Listen to tapes and discuss them. Listen to lectures or sermons and discuss them. Or just discuss. Just get going on your spiritual journey together. I am a real believer in the fact that if you look for God, you will find him. And if you and your partner look for him together, you will find him and a better relationship together in the process.

This spiritual dimension is overlooked by many. In fact, it's been my experience that most people come to God by the process of elimination—nothing else works! But when this priority is working, a most incredible centering and balance occurs in a person's life. Being at peace with God makes you at peace with yourself.

Over the years I have suggested with surprisingly good results that people use three steps if they are just beginning their search for God. It's a way of jump starting your spiritual batteries.

The first step is to pray to God. When you think about it, this is a logical step. As Creator of the physical world, God doesn't exist in the physical world, but in the spiritual. And if God is in the spiritual world, he can certainly hear if we talk to him. We can communicate with him about anything and at any time. Although this is a simple step, I have found it to be most rewarding for those who try it.

The second step is to read the great literature of the world. Start with the best-selling book ever, the Bible. Don't skip over this one. Read it in a good, modern translation. As you read it, pray to God that he will make himself known to you. The writings of C. S. Lewis are an excellent follow-up in your reading. Most people find their spiritual relationship with God becoming clearly outlined as they take this second step.

The third step is to talk with people who have searched for God and found him. Listen to them. Watch them. Take it all in as you continue the prayer and reading of steps one and two. I have known of only two people who started out on this three-step spiritual search and did not find what they were looking for. In each case one of the steps was eliminated.

When we search for a relationship with God, we will also find ourselves in the process. Some have related it to a God-shaped vacuum inside each of us. We try to fill that vacuum with every possible thing—relationships, money, chemicals, parties, vacations. But nothing fits, nothing satisfies. Nothing satisfies until that vacuum is properly filled with a personal relationship with God. Then we, as individuals, can function most effectively. Try it. You have absolutely nothing to lose and a spiritual relationship with God and yourself to gain!

The Second Priority: Relationships

The second most important priority in priority living is our intimate relationships. That special friend with whom we are staging a relationship emerges into this priority level. If it develops into marriage, it would include our mate, children, parents and friends.

This may be the toughest priority to see clearly and to cultivate day in and day out. This one may or may not give us immediate pleasure or responsiveness. We can't pay our bills with this one. It's only in the long run that we reap the benefits or the disasters that we have planted at this level, but we will definitely reap a harvest. Therefore, it is important that we share with our future mate the same priorities regarding relationships.

One area of family relationships that is often overlooked, and yet that has great bearing on a potential marriage relationship, is the commitment to our parents. The more I counsel the more I am convinced that this is the missing link of human relationships.

Once we move from the dependency relationship we have had with our parents and set up our own home, we move from obedience to honor. Obedience is easily understood, but the honoring of parents is fuzzy. We find ourselves caught between our need to be attached and our need to be separate. We want to be connected, but we also must stand on our own two feet as individuals separate from them.

A commitment to family is a commitment to honor our parents and our mate's parents whether we agree with them or not. Our responsibility is to honor them. We are not responsible for their response on the other end.

We honor our parents by seeking communication. Initiate communication with them, not just on special days, but keep in touch frequently.

We honor our parents by seeking their counsel and advice. This does not mean buying it necessarily, but seeking it.

We honor our parents by sharing the evidence of the positive marks they have made on our lives. We may have chosen to go a completely different direction than our parents wished, but they need to know what positive impact they have made anyway. We need to appreciate what they have contributed to our lives.

We honor our parents by recognizing that they are still growing, too. Their lives didn't come to a screeching halt when they finished polishing us up and sent us out the door.

We are different from our parents. We may even disagree with them, but we must honor them. If we are all locked up with anger, resentment or guilt in our relationship with our parents, we are less likely to form healthy relationships with those we date, and we are putting an unnecessary burden on any permanent relationship.

Because of the more immediate recognition and the absolute necessity of collecting enough cash to live, many men and women marry their vocations to the neglect of committed relationships. It is important to weigh this priority for yourself and your partner. If the priorities are out of sync, trouble is sure to follow.

About a year ago Barry, desperate to save his relationship, dragged Sylvia in to see me. They had not been together for ten months, but neither wanted it that way. They loved each other deeply. He felt certain that I could straighten out their problem. He exuded an inner strength within his macho frame that seemed to say his top priority was keeping in excellent shape. He was a gifted, yet driven, man. He was collecting well over two million dollars per year, and his investments were doing even better. His charitable gifts and energy were far beyond the norm. He was an exceptional man, making an unusual impact upon his world. But Sylvia said it well, "I respect your relationship with God and I admire your business accomplishments, but where do I fit?" I couldn't have articulated it more clearly. When you ignore priority living, someone will be painfully neglected. A commitment to important relationships is vital if we are to live life on purpose.

Choosing Love over Loneliness

On the way to committed relationships, there is a subtle culprit that sometimes blocks our making relationships a priority. The culprit's name? Loneliness. Many people have married because of loneliness and years later have divorced for the same reason.

Man is essentially alone, and this isolation cannot be dispelled by someone else but only by ourselves as we decide to love. It is the fear of love that is the root cause of every attitude and form of behavior that separates us from each other.

Many people try to relieve their loneliness through a change of scenery, a change of job or position or the purchase of new "toys" (clothes, jewelry, a boat, a plane, a car). One of the most common ways to handle the ache of loneliness is to change whom you are dating and move on to the next person quickly. When a relationship begins to uncover the many masks, it becomes threatening and painful to face. Therefore, it's much easier to move on to another more comfortable, surface relationship with someone else. But this only relieves the pain of loneliness temporarily, if at all.

The decision to choose love over loneliness has nothing to do with prosperity, possessions, playthings or the people who come in and out of our lives. But the decision is a people decision. Only other people can fill the loneliness vacuum, and only other people can adequately respond to our love. That is why it is so important to make relationships a priority in our lives. We must choose to open ourselves up to loving people. And that priority must be shared by anyone with whom we are considering a permanent relationship.

The Third Priority: Community Responsibility

In their book *Habits of the Heart*, Robert Bella et al. talked about a potentially destructive aspect of the American family. Although the American family was once a powerful social

145

force, contributing to the needs of the community, it has now become more of a haven for hiding—a place to get away from society. It is a dangerous "haven" because it promotes isolationism and self-centeredness.

In the seventeenth and eighteenth centuries the American family was highly involved in the culture at large. In rural settings families pitched in to help each other build houses and barns. Communities built their churches together. When one family was in need, others were there to help. Times have indeed changed. The word "community" once described interpersonal relationships within a certain geographic location. Today "community" is simply defined by geographic location.

A recent term that describes the new American family is "cocooning." It indicates the goal of our families to build all that we need within the walls of our own homes, epitomized by home entertainment centers that include large-screen televisions, VCRs, hot tubs and environmental control units. In Orange County, California, there is a restaurant service that will deliver food from the finest restaurants in town in thirty minutes or less. All of this so that we can avoid the presence and pressure of other people.

However, the irony is that we need the presence and pressures of other people. We are not created to be isolated in our own little cocoons. The third critical priority is a commitment to community responsibility. We need to be actively involved in the lives of other people; we need to be actively involved in our community. We can do this by voting, being a caring neighbor and participating in community service groups. Some of us have a natural outlet for interpersonal responsibility in a close, extended family. But, unfortunately, for most of us that, too, is becoming a thing of the past.

I think one of the best ways we can become actively involved in our community responsibilities is through our local church. There is no greater organization for social good than the church. The church is a place where people are committed to each other and to the community around them. The church takes care of the rich and poor alike. It gives a family a fuller reason for existence.

Any relationship that becomes so ingrown that "cocooning" is its goal is doomed for failure. We can only look at ourselves for so long. A commitment to community responsibility can insure greater growth in a relationship.

A Final Word

As with the interests and values we looked at in chapter five, we must assess our own priorities as individuals. And we must share with any potentially lifelong partner a commitment to the same priorities. It's hard to make and maintain commitments in light of a culture that prescribes a life of convenience. But the commitments to God, relationships and community responsibilities give meaning to our lives. They give us purpose; convenience offers only eventual decay.

14

Creative Conflict Within Commitment

Adrienne, a seemingly confident executive secretary, spent hours strategizing how she was going to tell Don she didn't want to marry him in six months. Several hours of prayer, consultation, writing it out and practicing in front of a mirror were all lost when she faced Don. "I just couldn't hurt him!" The thought of confrontation knotted her stomach. But the pain that might have come from the explosion of Don's anger cannot compare to the immeasurable pain that both Don and Adrienne will certainly face later.

I have watched people exhaust themselves trying to create smooth waters—a no-hassle, no-conflict, no-harm-no-foul relationship. These people will say anything, do anything and sacrifice everything to keep the other person happy and therefore have peace in the relationship. But the real question begs to be asked: is that really a peaceful relationship or is it merely a drugged one?

While some relationships ignore and evade conflict, others live in it. These people seemingly can't talk without fighting or arguing.

No matter how we choose to deal with it, conflict is inevitable in a relationship. Some experts say the average couple fights three times each day, with at least one major fight each week. Why do we have to have so much conflict? Why can't life be easy and smooth? It is because we are too different with different views of life, ourselves and others.

The way we deal with conflict will determine the health of our relationships. A relationship cannot exist without commitment, and commitment is matured by handling conflict properly. While counseling a couple, I am always searching for conflict and how they resolve it. If they are working through their conflict, their commitment is growing. If they are ignoring their conflict or fighting unfairly, no genuine commitment is even possible.

Conflict can be either cruel and crushing or creative and constructive. *Cruel conflict* is set up like a war, to inflict pain on the enemy. Cruel conflict twists resolvable conflict into damaging conflict, breaking down relationships. *Creative conflict* translates conflict into deepened commitment, which builds up a relationship. Commitment deepens when both partners demonstrate that they are more willing to resolve than run.

Conflict is like a brick. It's neutral and normal. In itself, it is neither good nor bad. That brick can be used constructively by building with it or destructively by bombarding someone with it. The choice does not belong to the brick; it belongs to the mason. We are the masons. The end result of conflict is completely dependent on what we do with it.

We all naturally bring our own bag of problems into our relationships. As these problems are let out of the bag, conflicts will occur. What do we do with them? How do we handle them? First, we must identify them.

Causes of Conflict

I see three major causes of conflict: rituals, rights and responsibilities. Rituals are those matters that reflect our own personal history and therefore determine how we respond to life. Rights relate to self-centeredness versus other-centeredness and so set a pattern of how we respond to other people. And responsibilities are those outside forces that complicate the process.

Rituals

I have a friend who habitually fought with his wife over dirty clothes. Instead of putting his dirty clothes in the laundry basket, he would leave them lying around the home. This turned into a major issue. So they worked out a compromise. He jokingly told me when I got married, "Listen, pal. Here's a plan that will work. Anything within three feet of the basket is in!"

Rituals are those practices we have nurtured and developed over a long period of time, perhaps our entire lives. These practices become so ingrained that they, in fact, become rituals.

Some of the rituals at the root of conflict are *habits*. We all have different ways of doing things. And some of our ways are just different enough to drive another person crazy, especially when we are together a lot. We like different foods, entertainment, clothing and cars. We have contrasting views on neatness, what times meals are served, what we do when we get home from work (talk, rest, read the paper, jog, work out). We have strange little idiosyncrasies like chewing ice, biting fingernails and drinking warm diet Coke for breakfast. Some people brush their teeth before they eat breakfast; others do it afterward. And on and on.

We rarely ever talk about someone else's habits because that would be rude. And if we do talk about them, it can easily turn into a fight because habits are so personal. They invite defensiveness. However, we have only two choices in the matter. Either we genuinely learn to live with our partner's habits, or we talk about them. It is not legal to brood about them.

Other rituals at the root of conflict come from our *back-*

ground. We each were raised differently. Our families are different. Each family heritage is unique. Some families are open and communicative; others are selective about their communication and still others are closed. Ethnic backgrounds really come into play here.

Our religious heritage and education are other factors that make us unique individuals. We become enmeshed in our own uniqueness and expect other people to be like us, think like us, act and respond like us. When they don't, we get ticked off. "What d'ya mean you don't like baseball? It's an American heritage!" Some people like baseball, others like ballet, few like both. Some people read, most watch TV. All of these are potential and normal sources of conflict.

Other rituals at the root of conflict come from our *beliefs*. Our beliefs concerning politics, war and peace, and liberal and conservative philosophies are no small matters. I once counseled a young couple who, because of their backgrounds, held diametrically opposed political views. He was from a poorer and more liberal family. She was from a wealthy, conservative home. Boy, did the sparks fly at election time! They had to work out a plan to air and discuss their individual positions. Communication, as we will see, is the key.

Rights

"I'm easy to get along with—just as long as things go my way." Isn't that the truth? We have such a hard time believing there are other valid positions than our own. We strongly feel that we have the right to be heard and obeyed. One of the commonest sources of conflict lies in our unwillingness to relinquish our "rights" for the sake of peace, harmony and love.

Many relational problems arise out of our own sea of expectations. We expect our partners to respond the way we expect them to respond. And when (not *if*) they don't, conflict will certainly follow.

152

I once counseled a two-income family who had a very sensible agreement. They shared the responsibilities for cooking and cleaning dishes. Their plan was simple. When one cooked, the other did the dishes. However, a problem occurred on the nights he was to do the dishes. He washed the dishes, all right. The problem was that he did them just before he went to bed. And it drove her crazy! If she went into the kitchen after dinner, she had to look at dirty dishes. As we counseled, I asked her one question, "What did you expect?" I explained that as long as she expected the dishes to be done earlier, she was going to harbor anger. But when she relented by allowing him freedom to do the dishes on the same night they were dirtied, but at the hour of his choice, she began to feel less internal conflict. She changed her expectations.

At the heart of the issue of rights and expectations is the belief in our American value system of *me, mine and my way*. What it boils down to is plain ol' selfishness. We all have it; it comes with being human, especially an American human in the twentieth century. We unconsciously feel that life and other people were created for our entertainment, fulfillment, growth and pleasure. But real life doesn't work that way. As stated in the beginning, it doesn't take long in a relationship to discover that you are dating a person very different from yourself, a person who also thinks that things should go his or her way. Serious conflict begins when two people advocate two different ideas about life. The goal is to discover that, despite our partner's apparent insanity, he or she is a person, too. And we need to see and do things his or her way as well.

Responsibilities

As if a relationship weren't tough enough on its own, we have responsibilities to outside influences that can create enormous conflict. Let me present four of these culprits to you. The first is *family and friends*. Do you want to know how much conflict family and friends can create? Try to plan a wedding. Everyone has demands and desires for *your* wedding. But you don't have to plan a wedding. Try to get engaged and ask for your family's and friends' opinions, or just ask their opinion about someone you're dating. Now, we're talking major stress. Family and friends may try to tell us where to live, what to buy and what to believe. This creates stress as we decide whether or not to follow their advice. Sometimes our partner will think that we are too strongly influenced by family and friends. And sometimes we are.

A second culprit is the real "F" word—*finances*. Nothing can cause more stress in a relationship than finances, even if you have enough money. Many think that getting enough money will satisfy their financial worries. Wrong. Not having enough money will certainly cause conflict in a relationship, but after we get money, another set of problems arises. How do we spend it? How much do we save? Do we use credit? Our differing values come into play. I might enjoy having an expensive meal at a nice restaurant, while my wife may think it is a waste.

I know a couple whose different values about money initiated an interesting conflict. They were catching a flight out of town, and when they arrived at the airport, the man hailed a skycap to take their luggage. The woman got very disturbed. She could not understand why he would waste two dollars when all he had to do was take the luggage inside to the counter. The problem was conflicting values about money. It was worth two dollars to him to avoid a long line, but she would rather have saved the money by standing in line. Money will cause conflict. Count on it!

Another outside influence that will cause conflict in a relationship is our jobs. This should not be surprising since we spend at least one-half of our lives at our jobs. Many of us have the lofty goal of "leaving the job at the office." While that is a wonderful ideal, it is not always plausible. Relationships at work are deep and affect us greatly. Sometimes we only bury work problems so that they get to us anyway. We have to expect our jobs to influence our lives at home, but serious problems occur when we have no life other than our jobs. In many modern relationships, men and women have staked much of their identity on their careers. When things do not go well at work, things are often not well at home. We have to remember the priority of our relationship at home.

The final outside influence that causes conflict is one that none of us can avoid. It is a devious little culprit. In fact, technically it is not even an "outside influence." But it seems we have so little control over this culprit that I'm going to treat it as an outside influence. The culprit? Our emotions. Don't you wish things didn't bother you? Don't you wish you didn't get your feelings hurt so easily? Don't you wish you didn't get jealous?

Emotions. If only we could deal with them better. But who knows what to do? When we try to control our emotions, people tell us we're denying them. When we express them, other people say we need to learn to control ourselves. Or perhaps your partner tells you, "You shouldn't feel that way," as if you just happened to select a particular emotion out of a grab bag. Our emotions often feel like little enemies hidden in our gut with the goal of sabotaging anything good that comes into our lives.

Our emotions will be the root of many conflicts. But as we discussed in a previous chapter, we must learn to express our emotions, especially to the person we love. That is the only way to defuse the potential time bomb within us.

Creatively Handling Conflict

After looking at the causes of conflicts, I begin to wonder how we ever get along. Sometimes I am amazed that we don't have more conflicts. The question is, what do we do with the conflict we have?

A welder once told me that if he took a strip of broken iron and welded it back together properly, it would be stronger than it was before. Creatively handling conflict is the same. If we work through our conflict well, our relationship will be stronger than it was before. Creatively handling conflict demonstrates mutual commitment. It shows we care enough to work through the rough spots.

What does creatively handling conflict entail? When we are resolving conflict, we must always be asking, what is our goal? What are we trying to accomplish? Cruel conflict has a win/lose mentality. Whenever there is a winner, there must always be a loser. In a relationship, we don't want to have losers. No one should get damaged. The goal, then, of creative conflict is win/win. Both sides come out on top. The idea of creative conflict is not for me to get my way or for you to get your way, but for us to find peace and harmony in the midst of our differences.

Consider two things to handle conflict creatively: approach and attitude. Our approach is a product of our personality, background and preferences. Our attitude is a product of our goals, maturity and humility.

Our Approach to Conflict Resolution

Depending on your resource, you will find several different approaches to resolving conflict. All of these approaches, however, can be synthesized into two. One of my associates, Marty Scales, has titled these two approaches Win and Withdraw. A *win* is a person who deals directly with conflict; whereas a *withdraw* will do anything to stay out of conflict. All of us have both styles within us, but we will generally lean to one or the other. As you read the descriptions of each, try to identify your own approach and the approach of your partner (as well as friends).

I have a friend about whom many people say, "You don't have to wonder what he thinks or how he feels about a problem. He'll always let you know." That is the trademark of a *win*—he expresses his joys and frustrations. A *win* doesn't necessarily enjoy conflict. A *win* isn't always looking out for number one. Nor is a *win* always trying to get his or her way. A *win* simply hates internal turmoil and will therefore talk about a problem when one arises. A *win* isn't afraid to say, "I think . . ." "I want . . ." "I need . . ." "You are . . ." A *win* will lay the cards on the table and then say, "Let's talk."

A *withdraw*, on the other hand, hates conflict. He or she will go to great lengths to avoid conflict. A *withdraw* will rarely say, "I want . . ." "I need . . ." and will almost never say, "You are . . ." Like a *win*, a *withdraw* does not like internal turmoil, but a *withdraw* hates conflict even more. So a *withdraw* will stuff his or her frustrations into a can, evading, avoiding, ignoring and denying. A *withdraw* will enter into a conflict only when prodded and provoked, and even then he will look for ways to get out of it.

Each approach has definite strengths and weaknesses. The strength of the *win* is that issues get discussed. The *win* approach does not guarantee resolution, but at least there's a chance. Problems can't be resolved when they are hidden. Another strength of the *win* is greater mental health. A *win* has fewer unresolved tensions to creep up and haunt him. A *win* deals more directly with his problems.

The strength of the *withdraw* is found in a laid-back attitude. He or she is not as bothered by problems as is a *win*. Many times apparent problems are like water rolling off a duck's back. A *withdraw* can be more at peace with himself and with the world. This attitude is great as long as it is not confused with avoidance and denial.

Herein is also the weakness of the *withdraw*. When a *withdraw* is really troubled by his or her partner, he will stuff it away somewhere rather than talk about it. Then, the next

*T*he danger of withdrawing is that problems never get resolved; they only get revisited.

time he is angry, he will stuff that away, too. Before long, a pressure-cooker effect is established. Then one of two problems arises—an explosion, sometimes over a seemingly minor incident; or, most commonly, passive-aggression.

Passive-aggression is usually unconscious. It says, "I'll get you for that, but I'll do it in such a way that you could never accuse me of getting you." Passive-aggression is being conveniently forgetful; it's being late; it most often retaliates by "not doing" something. We all practice passive-aggression at one time or another. At times in the middle of a conflict I know that all my wife needs is for me to walk over, put my arm around her and say, "I love you." But my passive-aggressive side prevents me from doing it, and she could never accuse me of retaliating.

The danger of withdrawing is that problems never get resolved; they only get revisited. A wall is silently built in the relationship. The bricks are placed one upon another in a slow and methodical fashion over a period of months and years. Eventually, honest communication ceases because problems have not been addressed.

The weaknesses of a *win* are much different. A *win* generally has a more aggressive personality type. Therefore, a *win* is more likely to make conflict when there really is none. A strong *win* will talk about everything that is bothering him or her. And that is enough to drive anyone crazy.

A *win* must learn to be wise and prudent. Before bringing up an issue, he has to evaluate the results. Will it make the relationship stronger? Will it produce better harmony, or is it me just trying to get my way?

If I were to vote for the better approach to creatively handling conflict, I would have to vote for the *win*, with a warning. The *win* is more likely to have intimate communication because he or she is not afraid to deal with pertinent issues. However, a *win* must be tactful and must use wisdom. I encourage *withdraws* to address their conflicts more openly.

Conflict is not pleasant, but it is better than no communication at all. And that is the guaranteed result when we do not work with our problems.

Analyze your relationships according to these "approach combinations."

1. Win and Win: This is a good combination if the couple is kind. If their goal is peace and harmony, they stand a good chance of adjusting to difficulties.

2. Win and Withdraw: The task of the *win* is to kindly help the *withdraw* open up and discuss conflicts. I have a friend who is a *withdraw*, but his wife is a *win*. They have a family rule: it is considered an act of love for him to tell her what is bothering him.

3. Withdraw and Withdraw: I counseled a couple of *withdraws* whose marriage had regressed to simply being compatible. They didn't have major arguments, nor did they have great joy together. Their marriage was "just there." Their problem was that they never discussed any of their conflicts; they ignored them. And soon they ignored the heart of their relationship. A primary task for *withdraws* is to learn to deal effectively with conflict.

The Attitude in Conflict Resolution

We will fight. There is no way to stop it. The question is, how will we fight? Will we fight fairly and creatively or will we resort to cruelty? Our attitude in fighting will make all the difference in the world. Our attitude has to demonstrate that we care deeply for our partner and for our relationship. Our attitude is reflected in our goal. Are we looking for a win/win situation or is it really a win/lose?

When we place a high value on our partner, we have the basis for healthy conflict resolution. Good relationships are ones that deal with problems and are willing to compromise because they value each other. Great relationships are ones with the goal of peace and harmony, a peace and harmony that comes from reconciliation not avoidance.

A good example of handling conflict peacefully is found in the book of James. The writer is dealing with varied conflicts. Notice his advice concerning conflict resolution:

> Who is wise and understanding among you? Let him show it by his good life, by deeds done in humility that comes from wisdom. But if you harbor bitter envy and selfish ambition in your hearts, do not boast about it or deny the truth . . . For where you have envy and selfish ambition, there you find disorder and every evil practice.
>
> But the wisdom that comes from heaven is first of all pure; then peace-loving, considerate, submissive, full of mercy and good fruit, impartial and sincere.
>
> James 3:13-17, NIV

Can you imagine a relationship in which the couple took James' advice seriously? Our conflicts would be much easier to deal with if our goal were peace, if we were full of mercy, impartial and sincere. Our main problem in dealing with conflict is that we always want our way. An attitude of peace and harmony is one that is willing to relinquish rights. It says, "I don't have to get my way all the time."

A Final Word

It is important for us to know the causes of conflict so we can see it coming and avoid it if possible. And it is important to handle conflict creatively by a proper approach and attitude. But the one clincher that will make us resolve our conflicts is commitment. When we just don't want to deal with conflict, when we no longer feel like it, the only thing that keeps us "hanging in there" is our commitment to our partner and our relationship.

Conflict and commitment work off of each other. Conflict will occur in a committed relationship, but commitment will ultimately get us through the conflict. And that resolution of conflict deepens our commitment. So don't be surprised by conflict. Rather, expect it—and creatively handle it for a stronger relationship.

15

Commitment to Sexual Distinctiveness

When I do premarital counseling, I have one objective in mind: to help a couple establish a good attitude about their marriage. Our actions emerge from our attitudes. If our attitudes are healthy, our actions will be also. There are several attitudes I try to promote—attitudes about commitment, trust, conflict resolution, realistic expectations. One attitude I am particularly committed to is our attitude about maleness and femaleness, our attitude about sexual distinctions and our unique sexual needs.

I am convinced that as males and females we have distinct needs that stem from our maleness or femaleness. This chapter is devoted to describing those needs. But I have a problem. I am going to try to describe an attitude, and in describing an attitude the details sometimes get in the way. You may disagree with specific points in this chapter, but don't miss the forest because of the trees. If you catch the attitude about our sexual distinctions, you will catch a lot. In fact, you may catch enough to change your relationship from bad to better or from good to great. And if you commit to your responsibility in your sexual distinctions, you will establish great strength in your relationship.

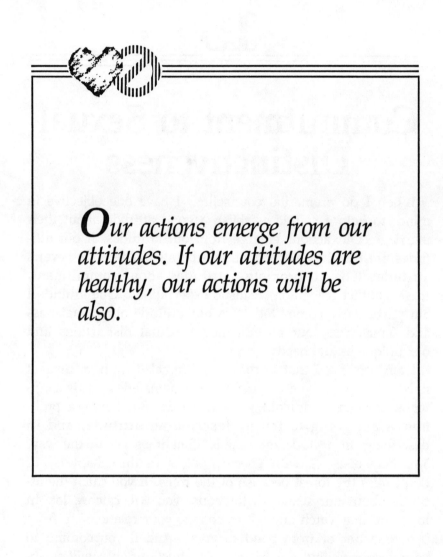

*O*ur actions emerge from our attitudes. If our attitudes are healthy, our actions will be also.

New Roles with No Rules

Our culture is in the midst of an exciting sociological era. So many changes are taking place. We are witnessing the emergence of two new subcultures—women and singles. Women have always been around, obviously, but they have never wielded so much influence. The singles' subculture is a completely new phenomenon. Never before in the history of the human race have we had so many unmarried people.

While emerging subcultures are of great sociological interest, they do pose some unique problems, not the least of which is how they integrate with our old social norms. Integration is quite complex. There is no easy formula to lay out a plan for women and singles to integrate into a society that is highly male dominated and family oriented. Yet women and singles are assuming more and more influential roles. Women are executives, police officers, fire(persons), laborers and heads of their households, and singles are parents and community leaders.

The result of these two, newly emerging subcultures is mass confusion. No one is sure anymore where he or she belongs or how he or she is supposed to act. An illustration of the confusion was seen in professional women's apparel in the late seventies when businesswomen adorned themselves with very male-looking business suits. A professor I once had who was the head of a liberal arts department, Dr. Janet Bennett, finally got tired of looking like a man and began to wear silk dresses to business meetings saying, "I don't want to look like a second class man. I want to look like a first class woman!" And that she was, socially and professionally.

Dr. Bennett evaluated the confusion concerning our culture's newly created roles with the following observation, "What we are dealing with is a predicament of *new roles with no rules*." And it will be a while before the rules are modified to go along with the new roles.

But what does all this have to do with commitment and relationships? It has everything to do with them because the confusion over the proper social behavior of those with new roles has led to confusion about healthy behavior in our relationships. Is there a "new role" for women within committed relationships? If so, what does it look like?

I am an advocate of traditional roles in a relationship. Now, by traditional roles I in no way endorse some absurd plan of chauvinistic male dominance. Rather, by traditional roles I suggest we recognize and admit sexual distinction and move on to serve each other in light of our male/female uniqueness.

The Traditional Model

The traditional model seems to be getting some bad press these days because it is misunderstood as an institution that holds women down and prevents them from growing. I would argue that the problem lies not with the model, but with a misuse of the model. The traditional model of a relationship has little to do with a woman's (or a man's) occupation or rights for equality; it has little to do with the management of the household. Rather, it has everything to do with the way we relate to each other as unique in our sexuality.

As I see it, the traditional model of a marital relationship is formed from three premises. It assumes first that we are relational beings and that our relational needs are met by other people. Second, the traditional model proposes that the most meaningful relationship between a male and a female is one that has a mutual lifelong commitment to honor, serve and love each other. And finally, the traditional model is constructed from the basic premise that men and women are different and that they have different needs in the relationship.

Just what are these different relational needs of men and

women? At the risk of oversimplification, I suggest that they can be narrowed down to two, one primary need for men and one primary need for women. I first came across the idea in Paul's letter to the Ephesians. In giving advice concerning marriage, Paul exhorts his friends, "Let each man among you *cherish* his own wife . . . and let the wife see to it that she *respect* her husband" (my own translation of Ephesians 5:33). In this passage Paul refers to Genesis chapter two concerning the union of a husband and wife. I believe that his appeal to the creation account indicates that he is talking about creation intent—innate needs within man and woman. The primary need for a man in a relationship is to be respected. And the primary need for a woman is to be cherished. (I think "cherish" more specifically communicates Paul's meaning here in this context of caring for and nourishing someone you love.)

Don't be deceived by the apparent simplicity of a respect/ cherish model. I have seen many marriages fail due to a lack of respecting and cherishing, and I have been delighted to witness failing marriages become restored by applying the principles of respecting and cherishing.

Women: Respect Your Men

Men and Masculinity

From the time a young boy is able to understand anything at all, our culture teaches him two very important notions: get ahead, achieve, accomplish, be something; and don't show emotion, don't cry, "suck it up!" These two notions will stick with him for the rest of his life, with greater and lesser degrees of influence.

It is no secret that men receive much of their identity and self-esteem from their achievements. Who a man "is" is based largely upon what he "does": his career, titles, rank, hobbies, sports, group affiliations. This is one of the reasons men are generally competitive. A man spends a large part of his life trying to live up to what he has been taught—get ahead. It is one of the strongest drives in a man.

Affirmation Through Respect

A man's desire for a woman's respect is so basic that it goes back to childhood. Have you ever watched grade school children play? Or, better yet, do you remember yourself that far back? (Some of us have further back to go than others.) It is humorous what little boys will do to get the attention and approval of little girls. They will show off and compete with other little boys, even get into fights, all for the affirmation of a little girl.

When my wife and I were dating, a headlight went out on her car. I went over to her apartment to visit one evening, and on the dining table sat a box with a new headlight in it. She then asked quite politely, "Do you think you could change my headlight for me?" Well, since changing a headlight was a "man's job," I naturally said I would. However, there was a problem that I failed to mention. I am a mechanical bimbo. So, out I went to save my masculinity. I discovered later that a headlight job should take ten to fifteen minutes. It's a good thing I didn't know that beforehand because it took me about an hour and a half. (I nearly took an entire fender off to get to the stupid thing!) When I finally completed my task, I asked her to come out and admire how perfectly her headlight now operated. She won my heart with her response, "You did that! All by yourself! Without a manual! You're terrific!"

Pam's affirmation for my little task meant a great deal to me. We laughed about the headlight ordeal later, but never about the issue of respect. As a matter of fact, when I received my master's degree, one of her graduation gifts to me was a coffee cup that says, "Atta boy"—our inside joke signifying her respect for my accomplishment.

A second illustration is more negative. A lady who was

separated from her husband and was considering divorce came to me for counseling. She told me her husband had moved out of their house and was having an affair with another woman. My immediate gut-level response was that her husband was a real jerk to walk out on his wife and child and go off with someone else. In our first session I sympathized greatly with her.

In our second session we began to probe the issues a little deeper. She told me, "I guess it's not that bad of a deal anyway."

"Why is that?" I asked.

"Well, I never really did like having sex with him in the first place. You see, I was never physically attracted to him." After more discussion I discovered that she had never offered to him the respect for his masculinity that he so desperately required. It is not surprising that he responded to the temptation of another lover. As I spoke with each of them, it became increasingly apparent that sex was not the issue at all. The issue was respect. He did not receive it from his wife. So when it was offered by another, he fell prey to it. Let me note here. I, in no way, condone her husband's extramarital affair. There were several more effective alternatives for him. I feel strongly about promise keeping. I only use this illustration to point out the gravity of the issue of respect.

A man's identity is built largely upon his achievements and accomplishments, and he needs to be affirmed for his deeds. The greatest affirmation a man can receive is from the woman he loves. She can hold the key to his strong identity. In a relationship, a man needs the respect of the woman he loves. It completes him and empowers him.

Exhortation for Women

I was once confronted by an attractive, talented and successful businesswoman who demanded of me, "Why do men have to be so wimpy and insecure? Just because I have been successful in business, most men I meet are either afraid of me or they want me to be submissive. Why can't a man accept the fact that I am his equal and that I have the right to challenge him when I think I need to?"

As we talked, I realized there was more at hand than merely "the right to challenge" a man. At the heart of her complaints seemed to be a deep bitterness, and she wanted more than the right to challenge. She wanted the right to assault. I tried to point out that what she desired contradicted the basis of any relationship. Everyone has the right to challenge and freely express opinions. But no one (male nor female) wants to be in a relationship where there is a constant power struggle. This is even more true, however, for a man, who needs respect. If a man feels that he is constantly being challenged and not respected by a woman, he is likely to respond in one of two ways: he might leave or he might become just what she can't stand, a wimp.

Women, please hear me. If you want to win the heart of a man, affirm his identity, his self-esteem. Give him respect for his achievements and accomplishments, respect for the way he loves you, respect for his masculinity. And in doing so *you will establish for yourself a position of strength*. You will set yourself up as more than his equal, as something better and more powerful than his equal; you will become his complement, just as he will become yours. And together you will rule your kingdom, your household.

Men: Cherish Your Women

Women and Femininity

While men in our culture are raised with the notions of achievement and control of emotions, women are raised with healthier notions. They are given permission to express their emotions; they are allowed to be more open and conversive about feelings and fears. Women are much more relationally oriented than men are. I believe this is a result of both innate talents and cultural orientation. It is part of the sexual uniqueness of women. And here we find the unique needs of a woman in a relationship.

While men attain their self-identity by means of their achievements and accomplishments, the identity of women is built largely upon how they *relate* to the world and to other people. It's not that accomplishments and achievements are unimportant to women. They are very important. But women see the world through more relational eyes.

Initially women are less interested in "what we have" and much more interested in "who we are" and "how we get along." I have counseled couples in which the woman earned more than $100,000 annually. These women all agree; they are more interested in the intimacy of their relationship than in their accomplishments.

It is for this reason that Paul said: "Men, cherish your wives!"

Affirmation Through Cherishing

The primary need of a woman in a relationship is to be cherished by the man she loves. A woman needs to know that she is a beautiful gift from God. She wants to be honored as a priceless treasure.

Sometimes we get very confused about these needs, especially in our day of heightened equality, which I do advocate. Remember, we are in a transition period in our culture where women face "new roles with no rules." We are working out the rules in the process. As we are working out the new rules, we seem to be hurting our male-female relationships in the process. Women, and men, are forgetting the very important reality that women are women, or that *women are ladies, too*! A woman at home does not want to be treated as a woman in the office. She puts on a different hat. She is no longer the competitive business person that she needs to be at the office.

In the early 1980s I attended a weekend workshop on male-female relationships. About forty men and women spent a Friday, Saturday and Sunday locked together in a dormitory where we participated in intensive lecture and interaction. Needless to say, we learned much about each other. I remember well one young lady who could be described as a radical feminist; she hated men. She strongly preached "the best man for the job is a woman." I can still picture her breaking out her guitar during our Saturday night free time and singing women's revolutionary songs. Well, I'm fairly open-minded, but by Sunday morning I had grown to dislike this woman, almost with a vengeance.

Then Sunday afternoon I had a change of heart. As the workshop came to a close, we all shared what we had learned from our weekend experience. This rough and tough lady slouched in her chair and began to reveal her heart. With tears in her eyes she said, "You know, this is the first time in my life that I have had such intimate interaction with men. I didn't know that men could be so soft and kind and caring." She then broke our hearts when she asked, "Why can't I find a man who will love and treat me tenderly? Someone who will put his arm around me and treat me like a lady?" I was crushed. I will never forget her. I was convinced that my theory was right. Women do have an innate need to be cherished and loved by the men they love.

Exhortation for Men

Men, do you want to win a woman's heart? Do you want to keep the woman you have? Do you want your relationship to grow stronger and deeper? If so, you must remember one simple and vital fact: the age of chivalry is not dead, especially in the hearts of women. A woman wants to be treated like a lady. She needs to be cherished. But on the other hand, she does not want to treated as if she were helpless and inept. She, too, needs respect. It's just that she will respond to being cherished first.

Just what does it mean to cherish the woman you love? What does cherishing look like? The first thing you need to know is that cherishing "feels" like something more than it "looks" like something. It is an attitude that you portray through your actions. It is the attitude by which you demonstrate to her how much you love her and how special she is. I'll offer six suggestions:

1. *Touching.* Touching seems to have much more value for women than it does for many men. So men often don't realize how important it is. When you touch the woman you love (hold her hand, put your arm around her, stroke her hair, offer love pecks), you are telling her something she needs to know from you, that you think she is attractive and adorable. It also symbolizes strength and protection from you.

2. *Participation.* You cherish her when you actively participate in your home and family life. Too many men are concerned only about their jobs and leave the homes to the women. They need to see you take an active role.

3. *Initiation.* You must adopt the role of initiator and not only responder. A woman can also be an initiator, but she will not feel cherished (protected and provided for) if you are *only* in the role of responder.

4. *Listening.* Show her you care by listening to what she has to offer. This is the number one complaint of married women. Listening includes asking questions and seeking input.

5. *Compliments.* When she looks good, tell her. And then tell her she looks good even without makeup. Never let her doubt that you find her desirable.

6. *Surprises.* Some people call this "romance." Bring her flowers, give her cards, take her to dinner. Let her know she is special.

Putting It All Together

In the Book of Beginnings (Genesis), the author writes that God created mankind in his image, an image composed of maleness and femaleness. Male and female are built to work in harmony, in a complementary fashion. I am convinced that a male-female relationship functions optimumly when it addresses the unique needs of males and females—when a man receives respect and a woman is cherished. These are the components for commitment.

But doesn't a woman also need respect and a man need cherishing? Yes, these are deep and important needs for every person. But I am after our *primary* relational needs.

There is a passive and active side of our relational needs that, when put together, form a perfect fit. Let me explain. Men have a passive need to receive respect and an active need to cherish. As much as a man needs to be respected, he also needs to cherish a woman. Likewise for women. A woman has a passive need to be cherished and an active need to give respect. She needs to give respect, as well as receive love.

The "fit" is perfect. It is the way we are built; it is innate; it is part of a plan. I have witnessed the success of this model over and over again. And when both parties are contributing, the relationship is strengthened and deepened because the more a man is respected the more he will cherish the woman he loves. And, the more a woman is cherished the more respect she will give to the man she loves. It works!

I was told the story of a man who played a terrible game of golf. When he would prepare to place his shot, he would always miss the ball several times before he would hit it. One day he found that his tee shot had landed directly on top of an ant hill. He walked up to the ball and started swinging. One stroke, two strokes, three, four, five, and he never hit the ball. As it turned out, every time he missed the ball there

174

was an ant massacre; in fact, it was quickly becoming the greatest massacre in ant history. Two ants were huddled over in a corner frantically trying to figure out how to survive the massacre when one of the ants told the other, "You know, if we don't get on the ball, we're going to die!"

It's the same way with our relationships. We have some unique sexual distinctions. Let's admit it and act accordingly. We need to commit to caring for each other with our sexual distinctiveness in mind. Respecting and cherishing is the way relationships are meant to be; it's part of the plan, and if we don't get on the ball, our relationship is bound to die.

16

You Gotta Call It Something!

When your relationship reaches the point where you must call it love or call it quits, you are probably experiencing some degree of stuckness. There is nothing abnormal about this. In fact, relationships can't be grown without experiencing some difficulties and some setbacks.

Stuckness is a relational limbo—two lives on hold. But it isn't as nice as that. Being put on hold sounds almost stable—no progression and no regression. But being "on hold" or "in limbo" is not being in a stable relationship. Far from it. If we are not growing in our relationships, we are going backward.

Not only are we going backward, we are, in actuality, gradually destroying our relationships. It happens in several ways. First, we will likely wound the other person in the relationship. As the frustration from not growing piles up, we will wound our partners either by what we do or say or by what we do not do or say. Second, we will wound ourselves. When we recognize the state of limbo and do nothing about it, our resentment very easily may become self-destructive. Third, we will warp our growth. This is true of both our relational and personal growth. Fourth, we will waste our time. Life is too short and relationships are too valuable to allow ourselves to be stuck in limbo going and growing nowhere.

This is precisely why we must call it love or call it quits. Either grow or go! Keep the relationship moving or move

*L*ife is too short and relationships are too valuable to allow ourselves to be stuck in limbo going and growing nowhere.

along! Keep it alive or bury it! But whatever we do, we must not allow our relationships to sit, soak and sour.

To call it love or call it quits means we must do three things.

1. *Clarify our personness.* We must clear up the confusion about who we are, and we must look, listen and learn all about the significant "other" in our lives. We must understand and appreciate the unique persons that both we and our partners are.

2. *Continue the process.* Once a relationship has been launched, we can't afford to rush the stages or, conversely, to get stuck in one of them. Instead, we must carefully move through the natural stages of intimacy with a definite strategy to win.

3. *Commit to permanence.* Permanence is not destroyed by the blunders of another person. Permanence refuses to be put off by the pain of conflict and communication. Permanence recognizes that strengths and weaknesses, compassion and conflict, passion and pain, happiness and hard times are all package deals. We cannot commit to one without the other. Permanence is a lifestyle of commitment.

Years ago I heard a wise professor say, "Even if you're on the right track, you'll be run over if you don't keep moving!" The same is true of a relationship. Don't let your relationship stop growing. You may call it love, or you may call it quits, but you gotta call it something!